THE CASE OF AMERICAN DRAMA

THE CASE OF AMERICAN DRAMA

BY

THOMAS H. DICKINSON, 1877-

EDITOR OF
"CHIEF CONTEMPORARY DRAMATISTS"

BOSTON AND NEW YORK
HOUGHTON MIFFLIN COMPANY
The Riverside Press Cambridge
1915

No man can quite exclude the element of necessity from his labor. No man can quite emancipate himself from his age and country, or produce a model in which the education, the religion, the politics, usages and arts of his time shall have no share. Though he were never so original, never so wilful and fantastic, he cannot wipe out of his work every trace of the thoughts amidst which it grew. Now that which is inevitable in the work has a higher charm than individual talent can ever give, inasmuch as the artist's pen or chisel seems to have been held and guided by a gigantic hand to inscribe a line in the history of the human race.

EMERSON.

PREFACE

THE purpose of this book is a simple one. In referring dramatic art back to the principle from which all art springs, it is expected to show the manner by which an American dramatic art may arise.

In these days of the collapse of the old theatre, and the Babel of new voices, each one advocating his own panacea of reform, it is appropriate to pause for a moment, even to look backward over well-trodden paths, in order that we may try old principles in the light of new practice. The one need of these days is standards. We have been so much cut off from the past that the rules of the old order do not satisfy us. And the new régime has not yet supplied its rules. We are all looking forward somewhat fearfully into the future, awaiting the coming of events, and recognizing that we have not the standards by which to judge the new when it arrives. When all other principles have been tried and have failed, or have brought but a dubious success, there will remain one principle of judgment that is always sure, a principle which has existed from the beginning, and by the operation of which, we may believe, destiny itself places the stamp upon the works of men. This is the social principle. No art can or will endure save as a part of the life of man. The life of man is the necessary substance of the life of art, and art draws its breath of immortality only from man. A living art must be incorporated into the life of man and be true to that life.

This raises no question of the artist *versus* society and enforces no social creed. A few years ago it was the drama of intellectualism that governed. To-day it is the drama of sight and "style" that is exciting the fervent bands of young workers. How are the values of these and other forms of drama (and by drama I mean everything that goes on in the theatre and much more) to be judged? Simply by the place they take in the " general heart of men." If they are indispensable to man's best interests as these are selected through the sieve of time, they will live. If they are not universally indispensable, and therefore organized into man, no joy of the moment, no stimulation of the instant whim, no illumination of the problem of the hour, will save them beyond their little day. In this book we are both old-fashioned and new-fashioned. We would go back to the inalienable principles of dramatic art as these have been worked out in the past in order that we may go forward to the service of a new drama of a new America. We would look back to sure principles in order that we may go forward to true discoveries. For from these principles there will come standards, and from standards will come safeguards and the certainties that underlie the art of a free people.

One word of warning may be permitted. When in

the following pages reference is made to the national institution of the theatre in America, it should not be thought that any particular type of theatre is in mind. This book is not an argument for the national subsidized theatre, for the endowed theatre, or for the experimental theatre. It is rather a study of the forces that may, in the fullness of time, bring forth an American theatre of a form that will be appropriate to the event. The writer gladly acknowledges the services of his friend Mr. Harold Gibson Brown in reading the proof of the book.

THOMAS H. DICKINSON.

CONTENTS

THE CASE OF AMERICAN DRAMA

CHAPTER I

THE NEW THEATRE IN THE LIGHT OF HISTORY

IT is difficult to do justice to our own times. Something over seven years ago the New Theatre was first announced to the nation. In due time it appeared and passed away. About it from the first was such a buzzing of comment and criticism, pointed and pointless, learned and literary, friendly and frankly malicious, that the institution itself has been lost in a cloud of words. The general impression strangely left was that the New Theatre had been a failure. This impression may be ascribed largely to the often recurring charge that the building was too large for its purpose. It was strengthened by the early closing of the experiment. I think the real reason for the impression of failure is that so far no one has told what the New Theatre really was.

Now in this study of the history and accomplishments of the New Theatre it will be desirable to omit any reference to the motives of the founders or the mistakes of the directors. Whether the former can be successfully impugned it is not necessary to ask; certainly the latter have been unduly magnified. To one who attempts to distinguish the achievements of the New Theatre from the mass of debate by which these have been surrounded, the New Theatre stands out a notable institution, a success by all it stood for and accomplished, and no less in its apparent failures than in its victories. According to any demand that the New Theatre should achieve the impossible, it was indeed a failure. But by the standards of reason, which come from a historical judgment, it is seen that it accomplished as much as any like institution in the history of drama has accomplished in a similar time.

A comparative study of present dramatic conditions with those of the past reveals nothing more significantly than the fact that essential conditions change but little from age to age; that the problems of one century may easily be stated in terms of the problems of other centuries. We have, therefore, ready to hand data for the understanding of the task laid before the New Theatre. There is nothing unique in the present awakened interest in drama. The evils of the traveling troupe, which we now think a peculiarly contemporary problem, were understood and corrected in Germany during the third quarter of the eighteenth century. Even theatrical monopoly is no new thing, for France fought and overcame a theatrical aristocracy a hundred years before Molière.

And the work of the New Theatre was no more and

no less difficult than similar tasks undertaken in various nations in the past. The first requirement for the accomplishment of such a task is that it be undertaken genuinely and thoroughly. No halfway measures can win any degree of success. And no insistence upon improving the play, while the player stands where he is, and audience and management remain unchanged, can serve the purpose. In such an institution the only honest course is the most difficult one. But even in this respect we get abundant light from a study of the past. When France and Germany began the reconstruction of their drama, interest in the problem was diffused among all classes, authors, actors, critics, men of affairs, and people at large. Such success as was secured came from coöperation of these classes. And so in England and America to day, as in France of the seventeenth century, and Germany of the eighteenth century, the play, the actor, and the manager are all reciprocally bound and their fortunes must rise or fall together.

It may fairly be said that the New Theatre represents a substantial advance toward a national institution of the drama in America. Whether that institution is to be a single centralized institution, or is to be distributed over the country in a variety of forms and in many centres, in the fashion of independent local repertory theatres, it is clear that such an institution is necessary, and that it has not as yet been secured. In essaying once and for all the centralized institution, the New Theatre did much to clarify the problem of the type of institution we are to have.

For Anglo-Saxon countries to-day the national theatre must be predicated on a quite different theory from that which obtained in France and Germany. Both these nations established their theatres by aristocratic fiat, and both of them incorporated them in institutions supported by the state. Such a source and such a form are inconsistent with the democratic principles of Anglo-Saxon peoples. But the difference is more apparent than real. Whatever the source, the national institution of the theatre in Germany and France has become a democratic thing. It has kept step with the times because the organizers of the state theatres gave it an impetus to a dramatic art not only worthy but free. And as to form the important thing is, after all, not so much the source from which the theatre comes as the sanction that gives it continuing life. Even a prince cannot command the artistic approval of his subjects, and a theatre stood or fell under an aristocracy, just as it must do under a democracy, through the approval or disapproval of its patrons. The last word in dramatic art must always be with the audience, whether that art be subsidized by a court or a wealthy man of affairs, or whether it be dependent upon the patronage of the people themselves. We are likely to forget this, and doing so to magnify the differences between the status of dramatic art in one

country and that in another. In all essential respects
the conditions of being of a national theatre to-day in
America are the same as they were in France and
Germany of a century ago.

It is clear that a national institution of the theatre
cannot be built in a night and a day. Its growth will
be one of social organization on the one hand, and of
artistic functioning on the other. In such a process,
at best a deliberate one, an ounce of doing is worth a
pound of theory. To this doing the New Theatre reso-
lutely set itself. It is for this reason appropriate to
survey the accomplishments of the New Theatre in
the light of the history of similar movements.

THE RECORD OF THE NEW THEATRE

Just at what point the practical project of the New
Theatre started it is not necessary now to inquire.
As an artistic conception it was nursed in the brain of
Heinrich Conried, a director who had been reared in
the old school of drama and in the school of opera.
Conried died before the project was put into execution,
but he left upon it many marks of his planning. The
New Theatre opened in the fall of 1909, under the di-
rectorship of Winthrop Ames. It lived for two seasons,
the final announcement of the abandonment of the
experiment coming in the fall of 1911. During the
history of the New Theatre the following things were
done: —

First: A building was provided, in every way worthy

architecturally to be the headquarters of an American drama.[1]

Second: A company of players was gathered together that as nearly as possible represented the equilibrium, the diversity, and the stability of the ideal stock company. The director stated the purpose of securing actors of versatility, of stellar magnitude, of sympathetic personality; in other words a company as nearly as possible of the class of the Lester Wallack and A. M. Palmer stock companies of bygone days. In spite of some mistakes, he succeeded admirably.

Third: The status of the players was raised well above the standards of commercial companies to a place commensurate with the real deserts of the profession. Players were provided with sufficient intervals of rest to keep their art vital; their rôles were diversified and they were given increased responsibility.

[1] In this summary many matters of mere detailed criticism will be avoided as not relevant to the larger issues. Much has been made of the mistakes in repertory, in casting of plays, and in modernization of ancient masterpieces. These criticisms may be just without invalidating the principles upon which the theatre was conducted. The matter of the size of the building, for instance, serious as it was, is more a matter of detail than of principle, and should not be permitted to take too large a place in the consideration of the achievements of the institution. Though one can never be sure how much the great size of the auditorium had to do in starting the psychological current against the theatre, it is a safe presumption that, theatrical conditions being what they are, the first "new" theatre would hardly have lasted more than two years in any event. The blunder in size seems to have grown out of the fact that from the start there was some confusion in Conried's purposes between imitating the Opéra of Paris and the Comédie Française. Of the first Napoleon had said that it was the vanity of France, while the latter was its glory.

Fourth: A balanced repertory was selected, representing, as nearly as the exigencies of the first season would permit, the claims of different periods of English drama and the strongest present tendencies on the Continent.

Fifth: Substantial steps were taken, in the words of the director, "to avoid the artistic disadvantages of purely commercial management, and still to remain self-supporting." One of the most important of these was the insistence upon frequent changes of bill.

Sixth: The function of the theatre as an instrument of formal social culture was accepted in a series of East Side subscription performances, presented with all the perfection of the regular performances, at prices ranging from ten to fifty cents. It is said that there were over forty thousand applications for tickets for the first performance.

· Seventh: The function of formal education was put into practice in the second season, in a series of four lectures, with histrionic illustrations, on the development of the English drama, delivered by Professor Brander Matthews, of Columbia University.

Eighth: Contemporary authorship was encouraged in the production of plays that the commercial manager would hardly venture to produce; one such play was Sheldon's "The Nigger." The New Theatre produced "The Blue Bird," after it had been declined by several managers.

Ninth: The directors of the New Theatre recognized

that a national theatre should not be merely a city theatre; that as far as possible it should distribute its influence. This was done through a spring tour which took the company as far west as Chicago, in a typical selection from its repertory.

Tenth: Recognizing the danger of monopoly in art, the New Theatre management provided that, after a play had been held for a certain length of time in the repertory, arrangements should be made for leasing it out to commercial managers for tours of the country. Care was taken to guarantee that the traveling production should be of equal standard with the original.

Eleventh: Partly through necessity,—for the repertory was hard to fill, — and partly through principle, the New Theatre was hospitable to actors and productions which were not a part of the programme of the theatre. Such hospitality is in the spirit of the German theatres, and, discreetly managed, can do much to encourage cordial relationships among different theatres.

Ignoring, as we justly may, isolated mistakes in administration and neglecting also the charge of snobbishness that was early brought against the theatre, we have in these eleven counts a respectable catalogue of experiment and achievement. Let us now, for the purpose of a more constructive criticism, look at the history and principles of similar institutions in other lands.

THE COMÉDIE FRANÇAISE

The Comédie Française of Paris was the product of monarchy. It is one of the few institutions of the kingdom of France which have withstood the shocks of revolution and have maintained their integrity under the Republic. Its history and methods of work can for our purposes be compressed into a few words. The Comédie Française was established by act of Louis XIV in 1680, through the union of the three Paris companies: Molière's company, called the King's Company, which had been established at the Palais Royal; the company of the Marais Theatre; and the company of the Hôtel de Bourgogne, called the Royal Company. Of these the first and second had been in combination since the death of Molière in 1673, and the rivalry between the combined companies and the company of the Hôtel de Bourgogne was only ended by the establishment by royal decree of the Comédie Française.

Upon the establishment of the new company, the system of control which had existed under Molière and which had been common both in England and France was continued in the new company; that is, the actors were given practical, responsible control of the fortunes of the theatre, subject to the royal prerogative as represented by the director. Such a condition has persisted to this day, outliving all revolutions and adapting itself to the republican as to the monarchical régime. The institution is now practically governed under the democratic system, worked out by Molière in the time of Louis XIV. The modern regulations, based closely on the ancient law, date back to the famous Edict of Moscow of 1812, signed by Napoleon and modified in unimportant particulars in 1850 and 1859.

Sarcey has said that the control of the Comédie Française is in the hands of a system part monarchical and part democratic. The democracy is represented by the actors, who in a body of twenty-four control the inner conduct of the theatre. These sociétaires, acting sometimes through committees and sometimes by authority delegated to a single person, select the plays, engage the associates, produce new plays and rehearse old ones, and share the profits of the theatre. All these activities are carried forward under an administrator, who typifies the monarchical side of the government of the Comédie. The sociétaires control the internal management of the theatre. The administrator, who is responsible to the Minister of Fine Arts, represents on his side the Government of France in relation with the institution. The position of the administrator-general is an exceedingly delicate one, for the reason that the line between the internal and external administration cannot be rigidly drawn. Experiment has shown that the conduct of the Comédie usually reflects for any given time the character and force of the administrator. Success in this position is gained through meeting and reconciling the critical opinion of the sociétaires and the public.

An interesting feature of this dual system of government is pointed out by Sarcey. It has been found that the democratic arm of the organization, represented by the actors, enforces the claims of tradition and conservatism. The monarchical part of the organization, on the other hand, represented by the administrator, is the radical and innovating arm.

What, now, are the characteristic features of the Comédie Française that demand consideration?

First: It represents the state as pledged to the support of the best dramatic art. The Comédie Française is a standing charge on the nation to the amount of 240,000 francs a year. In addition, the nation provides the building and its museums, libraries and facilities free to the comedians. The reserve funds supply ample guaranties for pensions. No profits can accrue to the Government, but all surplus is divided among the sociétaires, according to the value of the share held; or is placed in the reserve funds. In the year 1906 the expenses of the Comédie Française exceeded 1,600,000 francs. In France, therefore, dramatic art is recognized in the same way that education is recognized in America; that is, as a thing meriting financial support. This support is not a gratuity; in return for it, the Comédie is expected to serve the nation in the different ways to be indicated hereafter.

Second: The Comédie Française is the great mother

of the drama in France. It is the institution which
conserves in integrity the dramatic traditions of the
nation from the time of Molière and Corneille and
Racine onwards. It provides and perpetuates the
standard by which everything in authorship and acting is judged. Nine out of ten of the great authors
have sooner or later found a place in the Comédie
Française. Not quick to accept the new thing, it has
used the Odéon and the Gymnase Dramatique as
vestibules to its portals, and a play which achieves
success elsewhere is likely ere long to be impressed into
the programme of the Comédie. It has also monopo-
lized the services of the greatest actors. With it have
been associated with few exceptions the greatest figures
in the history of the French stage in two centuries.

In a strict sense the Comédie has been a monopoly
theatre. High as it stands as a monument of French
drama and great as have been its services to the nation, its prosperity has been gained somewhat at the
expense of the tributary theatres of Paris and the provinces. In its case centralization of art has gone so
far that distribution has suffered. The performance
of some of the classics outside of the Comédie Française is contrary to tradition. Outside plays and actors
are subject to continual command. The result has been
that the Comédie Française makes the best show for
French drama at the point at which it is most in public
view; that while feeding the centre it has impoverished
the circumference. It is against this condition that

revolt has been made during the last generation. This revolt does not, however, invalidate the services of the institution in providing and enforcing standards.

Third: The Comédie Française is to-day the chief example of a theatre substantially controlled by its actors. The increased responsibility attached to the calling has conduced both to the dignity of the actor's position and to an elevated standard of dramatic art. Self-management of productions is made possible through the fact that players are engaged to play only certain types of rôles.

Ordinarily a player can expect to be assigned a rôle only in the class for which he is engaged. It need not be said there are positive disadvantages in this system which the French have not been long in finding out. There are also some clear advantages. The first of these is in favor of the actor to whom a refreshing variety in rôles is practically guaranteed. No less important is the advantage to the company as a whole. In no institution in Europe is there as extended a tradition of coöperation as at the Théâtre Français. As a result this company stands as a model in the art of *ensemble* acting.

Fourth: The repertory of the Comédie Française is characteristic of the exclusiveness of the French people. Few foreign pieces find their way to the stage of this theatre. But, lacking the impulses from beyond the border, the repertory is all the more representative of the history and traditions of the French theatre. Having "a continuity of interest and a solidarity of emulation," the sociétaires have been able to maintain the integrity of the ancients before the attacks of the moderns. Between these two there is inevitable conflict.

"The necessity of keeping the old repertory on the boards side by side with the new plays is one of the glorious conditions of the Théâtre Français and at the same time it is one of its burdens," quotes Claretie, from a report of the administrative committee of April 6, 1852. On the other side is the statement of Dumas père, that "The first theatre in France exists to keep green the memory of our old glories and to bring into relief our new glories, but it cannot offer a channel wide enough for the multitude of dramatic attempts, which are still groping their way in the night of art." In spite of the claims for the conservation of the old, there was under Claretie a very strong tendency toward the moderns.

Fifth: The art of the stage is recognized by France as one worthy of formal instruction. The young actor is not left to the haphazard precept and example of fellow players little more expert than himself, but by a system of expert tuition is taught the theory and practice of his art. Education in the art of the theatre is recognized as a charge upon the state. And the science of formal instruction in the technique of an art has nowhere gone higher than in the Grand

Conservatory of Paris. This institution is recognized as the stepping-stone to opportunity in the theatre. Upon receiving a certificate the graduate is sure of a position, and the graduate of first rank is permitted to appear on the stage of the Théâtre Français. The significant thing is that this institution is supported by the state. Following the example of the nation, some of the larger cities have their city conservatories which open to the city theatre, as the Grand Conservatory opens to the Comédie.

Sixth: In supporting the Comédie, France demands a direct and formal recompense in return. The indirect return is always there; in addition there are formal benefits that the Comédie can pay. The museums and libraries of the historic institution are open to the student of French dramatic history. The obligations of the Comédie as a formal social instrument in the drama are fulfilled through the official performances for students and state employees. During a year about one hundred and fifty thousand gratis admissions are distributed. As an arm of the state, the Comédie is expected to be discreet in its alliances, and enemies of the established social order can find no outlet on its stage.

Seventh: The great outstanding institution of the Théâtre Français undoubtedly exacts the price of majesty from the nation. But if it demands tribute it also serves as a model. In its train there have sprung up in the cities of France city theatres, subsidized by the city as the Comédie Française is supported by the nation, and serving the higher standards of the community as the Comédie serves the higher standards of the nation. All the way down to the city which supplies a subvention of about eight thousand dollars a year, each city recognizes its obligation toward dramatic art. And the provinces are not left without the stimulating touch of the larger institution, for, through the summer tours of the company, the art of Paris is taken even to the outlying provinces of the republic.

If during the last thirty years a way has been made for "free" theatres that can work in zones untouched by the theatres of tradition, this fact must be credited to the stable support of the best in taste through many years by the Comédie Française.

THE SUBSIDIZED THEATRES OF GERMANY

The awakening in dramatic art in Germany during the eighteenth century is strikingly similar to the awakening that is now taking place in English-speaking nations. So saying, one is aware that there is a very great difference between the material prosperity of the drama of the two nations at these times. Drama to-day is a very profitable business, but so far as the art is concerned, this prosperity is, or lately has been, more apparent than real. From the point of view of art, drama in Germany of the eighteenth century was as sterile as was drama in England in the nineteenth century.

It was not until after the middle of the eighteenth century that the tide began to turn. Up to that time there were only three dramatic companies of any standing in all the states of Germany. For the rest, drama was produced by traveling troupes of poorly paid actors, playing in poorly appointed theatres. The art of acting was at a low ebb. There were two or three great actors, but there was no pretense of *ensemble* acting. No German Garrick had yet appeared to represent the principles of a fine individual technique and to organize a harmonious machine of well-balanced players. The drama itself was artificial and without soul. It had no connection with current life, with true psychology, or with the German temperament. In the seventeen-twenties a heroic effort had been made by Gottsched and Frau Neuber, directors of the Leipzig troupe of actors, to raise the standards as regards actors, plays, and productions. The result was thoroughly to bind Germany to the influence of France. Paris became the capital of German drama of the eighteenth century, as it was later to be the capital of the English drama.

Such were the conditions when the Hamburg National Theatre was established in the seventh decade of the century. Thereafter the movement rapidly advanced until, by the beginning of the new century, the whole body of German drama had been changed once and for all. In this thirty years' renascence the names of many men, actors, visionaries, and authors

are met again and again, sometimes associated with
one theatre and sometimes with another. With the ill-
fated Hamburg National Theatre of 1767, there are
associated particularly four names, given in ascending
order of genius: Seyler, Löwen, Eckhof, and Lessing.
The first was a well-to-do and stage-struck merchant,
who happened to be first the chosen lover and later
the husband of a popular but capricious actress, Frau
Hensel, whose varying fortunes led him into many
ventures. The second was a literary amateur of the
stage whose visions went beyond his judgment. The
third was one of the first of the great actors of the
modern epoch of German drama, and the last was a
preëminent philosopher, dramatist, and critic of art.

Before the opening of the Hamburg National Theatre, Löwen had published a volume of "Theatrical
Writings" for stage reform, in which he had outlined
many improvements that were finally put into effect.
In his new order were to be: —

Stationary troupes.

Fixed theatres in great cities supported by the state.

Theatrical academies for the training of players.

Encouragement of original authorship.

The Hamburg National Theatre was established
under Löwen by twelve Hamburg merchants, of whom
Seyler was the leader. Its life was short. Löwen was
inefficient as a director, and dissension among the actors
soon brought the experiment to a conclusion. But the
venture secured a long life in history in a manner little

expected at that time. At the opening of the theatre,
Lessing, who then "stood idle in the marketplace," was
asked to serve as stage poet for the theatre. Upon his
refusal to do this, he was engaged to write its criticisms
and notices. In this one thing the directors builded
better than they knew. A theatre that is to fill an advanced place in the art of drama needs not only to
supply good plays, but also to supply to the people the
criteria by which elevated art is to be judged. Lessing
wrote sedulously on drama for a year, criticizing each
piece that was produced, studying its artistic and social
and national implications, and working out the criteria of a new, though admittedly German, art of the
stage. These "flying leaves" of his criticism, when
gathered together, formed that "Hamburg Dramaturgy" which is the foundation of the modern German
stage, and is the best expression of modern philosoph-
ical thought on the drama.

The Hamburg National Theatre failed miserably,
but, as in the case of many failures, success rose out
of its ashes. Lessing had always been larger than the
movement to which he was attached, and as author
of the "Laocoön," had already written his name high
in the lists of the philosophers of æsthetics. And all
the others who had been associated with this theatre
went forth to other theatres to try again, and all played
their parts in bringing the national drama of Germany
into being. Schröder, who had worked under Eckhof,
remained for a time in Hamburg and created the first

ensemble acting in Germany, and, following the slogans of Lessing against a weak slavery to the French classic drama, was the first to open up the German stage to the wonders of Shakespeare. Eckhof went to Gotha and by Duke Ernest was given charge of the first court theatre. There he spent the remainder of his life. Even the complaisant Seyler is heard of again in a better venture than any of these, the Mannheim Theatre, established in 1778 by the Elector Karl Theodor, as the first really independent and therefore approximately "national theatre." In this venture there were associated three young actors, Beil, Beck, and Iffland, who had served under Eckhof at Gotha and after his death were glad to put into practice the theories that they were there unable to execute. With this theatre there is associated the name of the great Schiller as manager and author. Meanwhile, the Vienna Burg Theatre was reorganized in 1776, as a modified court theatre; that is, it was supported by the court, but its management was left in the hands of the actors themselves. This, the system of the Comédie Française, was, after the overthrow of Seyler, next adopted by the Mannheim Theatre also, and the most important step in the elevation of the dignities of the actor in Germany had been taken. Iffland, one of the trio from Gotha and Mannheim, we find later as one of the most popular dramatic authors of Germany, and in 1796 the director of the new Berlin Royal Playhouse.

Thus, within thirty years the management of German theatres had been revolutionized, the player had been raised to a position hitherto unknown, and pure literature had joined hands with the stage in the persons of such preëminent figures as Lessing, Schiller, and Goethe. The establishment of national theatres in Germany was followed by a wave of revolution in all departments of the theatre. Goethe and Tieck and Immermann soon brought forward their ideas for scenic and production reform. The movement thus begun has continued for a century and a half with ever-increasing prosperity.

Let us summarize briefly the conditions in Germany which have been the outgrowth of the dramatic renascence of the end of the eighteenth century.

First: The drama is to-day recognized as a charge upon the state and upon the city. The movement began as a private thing in Hamburg. Soon it was taken over by official patrons, and in the nineteenth century municipalities began to provide their own theatres. The court theatres are usually under the authority of a director to whom is delegated complete control. When the control is kept in the hands of a prince, the result has not been happy, as the director is much more likely to be amenable to the artistic demands of the patrons than is a prince. From this point of view, the municipal theatres have latterly been of better artistic service to Germany than have the court theatres, for reasons connected with the popular

control which are not far to seek. Of the court theatres, the Berlin Royal Playhouse has not been con-
spicuous as a leader, for perhaps manifest reasons.
Like the Comédie Française in Paris the court theatres
of Germany have nurtured national taste in matters of
the art of the theatre to a self-supporting maturity.
The results of this have been shown during the last
thirty years in which the German theatre has thrown
off the leading strings of protection and has gone forward independent and self-supporting.

Second: The German modern theatre is based upon
the theory of the coherency of the arts. Lessing, in his
"Hamburg Dramaturgy," which has been the Bible of
German drama since his time, insists upon all the social
and æsthetic and national connections of the art of
drama. It has been the fact that German drama has
been on a parity with other arts that has kept the
stage alive. Lessing himself, who stood for the idea in
theory, in his own person exemplified it. He started
the fashion, and since his day the greatest writers of
Germany have not been ashamed of positions in the
great theatres. Freytag and Spielhagen and Heyse
have followed in the wake of their greater predecessors.
Modern German theatres also reach a hand to the
plastic arts and arts of design, and in the office of
régisseur, or director of scenery, have been found men
of eminence in German art.

Third: The German theatres of the eighteenth century, among many other forces then at work, helped

to crystallize a national consciousness. More than this, they found voices to give that consciousness speech. Lessing, in his vigorous epilogue to the "Hamburg Dramaturgy," expresses this prime necessity in any art, the need of a coherent national character. "What a simple idea to give the Germans a national theatre, while we Germans are as yet no nation! I do not speak of the political constitution, but only of the moral character. One might also say: The character of the Germans is to insist on having none of their own."

The man who wrote these lines was himself among the first to give the Germans a dramatic art representative of the character of the nation. But before this could go far, the lines of the frontier had to be drawn, and artists had to discover that, while patriotism may be "the refuge of the scoundrel," it is also the breath in the nostrils of the strong man. The author of the first "Storm and Stress" play, Max Klinger, expressed this idea: "Why model our theatre after French fashion when we are Germans, and as the tinsel with which the heroes of Racine are loaded is so alien to our character? Why after an English pattern, when we are very far from the exuberant, brilliant humor of this insular people?" When the real awakening came, it was German to the core, and the Germans discovered dramatic art simultaneously with the discovery of their national life.

Fourth: In repertory the nineteenth-century German stage managed to secure a catholicity that is found on no other stage in the world. Not only are the classics of Germany, Lessing, Schiller, Goethe, Kleist, given full consideration along with the prolific outpourings of modern talent, but the classics of other nations find permanent place on the best stages of Germany. Since Schröder introduced "Hamlet" at Hamburg in the eighteenth century, Shakespeare has been as often produced in Germany as in England, and from Germany have come many renovating influences into the Shakespearean tradition. The Spanish Calderon is only less at home in Vienna than in Madrid. This hospitality extends to plays of the newer order as well as to the classics. The stage at Munich has been the trying-ground of stage experiment, and Ibsen looked to Germany for the production of some of his plays before they were produced in his own country. Receptiveness for the new and foreign thing has been the chief force in keeping the German stage alive, along with a vigorous and deep nationalism, which, under what provincial forms it may manifest itself, underlies the entirety of the art of German drama to-day.

ORGANIZATION OF THE AMERICAN NATIONAL THEATRE

This hasty review will serve little purpose if it is not already apparent that its chief value lies in what it implies and suggests concerning American drama, rather than in what it expounds concerning foreign drama. Diverse as are the problems of the German and French stage from the exigencies of our local condition, we can find in the history and methods of their stages abundant material for study and emulation. The first thing that impresses one is the fact that, though the external formulas may differ, the internal values remain practically the same; that the problem in Germany a century and a half ago was different only in insignificant details from the problem in America to-day. There is a lowest common denominator in art and society as well as in arithmetic, and, when we reduce our problems to its terms, we are more than likely to reach definite conclusions.

It is clear from the study we have made of the national theatres of France and Germany that these are not planned to be self-supporting. Whatever may be said of the whole question of business in the theatre, and this we will take up later, it is certain that the institution that is to create the standards of a nation's drama must be raised above the necessities of support from earnings. It should also be clear that no nation can be expected to go forward to free and self-supported work of a higher order until standards have been supplied in stability. This brings us to the question of subsidy and the source from which it is to be derived.

As has already been said, in Germany and France the national theatres were established from above in those eras when such action was more natural than it would be to-day, and they have been bequeathed from an aristocratic past as charges on a democratic present.

But it is quite unlikely that democratic England and America will be ready to provide such institutions out of their own vitals for some years to come, if indeed they are ever ready to do so. There is left, then, only that power which is, as nearly as may be, the modern equivalent of the possessing class of the older order, in other words, the men of wealth of the present day.

There should be no alarm over this situation. According to the modern social philosophy it seems quite fitting that wealth should return to society benefits derived. There are reasons for believing that such a theatre would be established better by private means than by the state. The power of an endowment continues long after the special interests which have provided it have passed away. A government must be kept under continuing tribute; and, unless greatly safeguarded, an institution so supported is likely to find much of its power directed to keeping in touch with the temporal powers of politics.

As to danger of interference with internal economy on the part of the supporting power, it makes little difference whether the organizing power lies with the state or in private hands, so long as final judgment is exercised by the patrons. The Comédie Française is not an expression of the shifting political government of France or even of the little group of sociétaires, but of the enlightened patronage of the nation. In those German theatres in which autocracy is most rigid, least has been accomplished for the drama and for the nation, and genuine popular support is almost wanting. On the other hand, in those theatres both in Germany and France, in which the director depends most closely upon the critical support of his patronage, as distinguished from official support, the standards of artistic attainment are said to be the highest. The source of the subvention is of little importance so long as this reciprocal relation between patrons and director is maintained.

The danger of interference by men of wealth is even less than the danger involved in the autocracy of courts. Absolute subservience to the donating power would be as impossible here as subservience to the prince has been shown to be difficult in Germany. Money can start a theatre, but it requires patronage to keep it alive. Any desire on the part of the wealthy benefactors to control art would meet in America with the same unsuccess as under the autocratic rule of courts in Germany. The result would be simply that art would fly to other quarters where it could be free.

But, it may be asked, how can one depend upon the support of public patronage for an art when public taste is as yet uncultivated? For answer to this we must fall back upon a truism. The good thing will always find patronage among the many if it is supported by the few long enough to give it a foothold. In art as in government the judgment of things "in the long run" is a pretty safe one. What is necessary in our day, no less than in other days, is the providing of that machinery whereby standards of art may be kept pure. We labor under no illusions with regard to the theatre of the Continent. It is faulty enough. It must carry on a perpetual warfare against debasing forces. But at least it has the instruments for that warfare. These instruments, represented in the solid continuity of tradition of an uncommercial institution we too must secure in a form appropriate to our system of life. If through the maintaining of the standard a more distributed interest follows, and with it there arise the commercial instruments for the serving of that interest, we will be but living over again the experience of France and Germany. For the richest fruits of the supported theatres of Europe have grown outside the walls of these institutions.

Standards must come down from above. Any real contribution to the service of the American theatre must be quite unmixed in motive. The theatre that will supply our standards will not pay for itself. In this respect the hopes of the founders of the New Theatre were doomed to disappointment, as is shown by two different statements issued only two years apart. At the opening of the theatre, Director Ames stated that it was the purpose of the house to correct as many of the evils of commercial management as possible, while still aiming to be self-supporting. Two years later, in the semi-official announcement of the abandonment of the first building, and while the continuancy of the project was still in mind, it was stated that for the future a regular subsidy would be provided annually. This lesson is enforced by a study of the subsidized houses of Europe. In Paris, Berlin, Dresden, Vienna, where the clientèle is certainly larger than in New York, the peculiar public demands that are laid upon the theatres make them perpetual charges upon the state. Such an institution cannot be expected to be self-supporting. Indeed, it is almost as much of a contradiction in values to say that a national theatre should support itself as to say that the opera, or the museum of art, or even that the university should be self-supporting. It is almost axiomatic that when one of these institutions begins to pay for itself, it is serving its coffers so well that it cannot afford to serve art. Wealthy givers in the future should approach their benefactions in this direction with no misconceptions and with purposes clear and unmixed.

Granting that drama should be freed from the necessity of earning a profit, the question arises, How shall the theatre be organized that it may be of best social service? The answers of France and Germany to this question are somewhat unlike. The first nation represents the ideal of concentration of power and influence in the Comédie Française, whereas Germany represents the distribution of the benefits of these institutions over the empire. France better secures a single

institution which is the shining glory of the nation;
Germany, on the other hand, by its system better secures that variety of expression and social contact that
are necessary for any art that lies close to the life of
the people. Great as the drama of France is, there can
be no doubt that drama is the better handmaiden in
Germany. And this lesson may well be learned in England and America. Admitting the desirability of a
national theatre, Henry Irving long ago pointed out
the greater need of municipal theatres in the provincial
cities. London and New York are pretty certain to
provide some fare for all tastes. It is in the large cities
outside of these metropolitan centres that the lack
of a great art of acting and of great plays is most
seriously felt. The suggestion of Henry Irving, which
was made as a result of long study of the needs of English drama, pointed the way in which the first steps
for a new system of organization in England have been
taken. Not in London, but in Manchester, and Dub-
lin and Birmingham, the repertory theatre movement
started. The movement will undoubtedly continue
in the way that it has begun. Along with the continued call for a national theatre in New York or Washington, it is altogether necessary that there shall go
a movement for city theatres in the great provincial
cities, Milwaukee, St. Louis, Denver, if our progress
in things dramatic is to be substantial and sound.

THE PLACE OF THE ACTOR

If we compare the conditions accompanying the professions of the stage in America and on the Continent, we discover that the profession of the actor commands much less respect here than in Germany and France. We cannot be satisfied to have this fact explained superficially as due to the supposed character of the men and women who enter the profession. We must look for the explanation in the conditions governing the life and art of players in this country, and in the debased standards of the art of acting, which have grown out of these conditions. Such a study convinces the investigator that, of all those who follow the stage, the chief sufferer from present conditions, both personally and in his art, is the actor; and that the most lamentable result of the system of management now in vogue has been to debase, and almost to kill, the art of acting.

At this point the present awakening to better things on the stage is accomplishing least. Authors have for several years had the stage well under their control, and all the movements for the improvement of the stage are now beginning with the written drama. This is carrying far the progress of the play as a written document. The advance of play technique of the last two generations exceeded the advance in two centuries before. Plays are read in English in numbers exceeding anything known since the eighteenth century, and the publication of plays becomes greater each year. Plays are again taking their place as literature on the library shelves, and a dozen writers are now composing in English plays that will stand scrutiny beside the study lamp. But with this advance in the art of the play, the art of the player has not been permitted to go, and the conclusion is forced on one, that so far the development has been a one-sided development; that such improvement as has taken place has been a literary thing rather than a thing of pure drama. Kindred as it is to literature, dramatic art is not literature. It starts, not with the printed page, but with the expressive functions of the human body. It concerns itself more with the play in execution than it does with the play in formulas of word and action. In a word, a play is not a play until it is produced; it is its amenability to production that makes it a play, and the art of the player lies at the very centre of the whole art of the drama. In every era in which dramatic art has risen to high standards, the art of the player has been vigorous and respected.

The decline in the art of acting is to be referred back to the changes in production involved in the methods of the commercial theatre of the last two generations. In the necessary steps for the elevation of the financial status of author, manager, and actor, changes in production were introduced which made impossible the continuance of the old ideals of acting. With the introduction of the system of traveling troupes, many of the conditions that lie at the basis of every art were removed from the art of the player. These conditions are spiritual stability, sufficient leisure, and healthful variety in work. None of these things is secured under the present traveling system. Authors have benefited greatly through the control they are able to maintain over all companies producing their plays, and managers have reaped the fruit of centralization. Only the player has found no real improvement in his position. Blinded by the increased number of positions from the lowest class up to stellar rank, and misled by an erratic system of high salaries, the actor has supposed that his position was well enough. Meanwhile he has been gradually and surely losing his foothold in the stable ranks of the professions.

One result of the present system of production has been to crowd the actor's profession with a host of young players unprepared by training and study for the exacting calls of their art. These are the actors who crowd the offices of agents during the winter. On the side of art the loss has been considerable. For one thing, responsibility has been taken away from the actor, and turned over to the author and the business man of the theatre. The place that the actor takes as artist in the significant productive work of the theatre is now limited to his own part. He is not expected to have any interest in the larger issues of the production. The result has been that the actor has become an automaton, a kind of histrionic traveling man. Actors are year by year taking a smaller part in the productive work of the stage. The term "actor-manager" has been coined to apply to a certain kind of manager, nowadays seldom found; in the old days all the managers were actors. It is a good day for an art when its business is in the hands of the artists themselves.

The art of the actor has lost in technical variety. Technique no longer means even what it meant a generation ago. In some respects this is good; in others, it means that we are throwing away the accumulated profits of years of experience. The average player does not receive as thorough and varied a training as the average player secured under the stock system. To be an actor should mean to be a student of human nature, with facile command of all the organs of expression, and a soul flexible enough to adapt itself to varying calls. To-day it may mean these things, happily does in many cases, but it may mean also simply to belong to a certain "type" which may be bodily transplanted to the stage. The art of the actor has suffered greatly through naturalism, and through the increasing use of actor-proof plays, which, composed to "play themselves," are practical admissions of the failing fortunes of acting. The system of endless repetition of one play has much to answer for. It has brought the stage to such a pass that it may be said that the better a part is for a player's pocket, the worse it is for his art. A succession of failures may be better training than one success. The fire of creation soon leaves a part under the dreary load of repetition night after night for years. This necessity of mechanical repetition has been opposed by the continental players who have visited America. Tomasso Salvini absolutely refused even to play two nights in succession. Bernhardt and Duse carefully vary their bills. "There is nothing more detrimental to the actor," writes Modjeska, "nothing more injurious to the advancement and development of his art, than the constant shifting from one place to the other, and, what is still worse, the run of the same play hundreds of times, until the actor's work becomes nothing more than a mechanical and weary reproduction of his part night after night, and his only desire is that it may soon be over."

Serious as these conditions are when viewed from the point of view of the actor, they are seen to be doubly serious when viewed in the light of their importance to general stage conditions. No great art of drama can be built up except on great conceptions of playing. Indeed, great drama was never known to exist except at a period in which the art of the actor was vital. Past movements for the elevation of the stage in other nations have been pushed forward to success, not so much by the idealists and visionaries from other arts as by trained and expert players. Before he was a writer Molière was an actor. The dignity of the Comédie Française and reciprocally the dignity of acting have been maintained by the fact that actors have been placed in responsible charge of the institution. The reformation of German stage conditions was brought about by a handful of energetic players, Ackermann, Eckhof, Schröder, and Iffland.

If the movement for a dramatic renascence is to continue, it must proceed through a raised valuation of acting as an art. This is practically impossible of achievement in the present system of traveling companies. Not the least argument for the repertory system is that it provides an excellent training-school for players. This training is excellent in two directions, both highly necessary in these days. First, it trains the individual actor in many parts, as Irving had played six hundred parts in the provinces before he ventured to London. Second, in providing a stable company, it makes possible an *ensemble* art, after the manner of the old companies of Molière and Garrick, art instruments of wonderful precision, balance, and harmony, and of the fine companies of the stock days in New York.

The endowed theatre alone can afford to take the first step in the accomplishment of these ends. This step taken, other managers can follow. Another thing that the endowed theatre can do is to restore dignity to the art of acting by restoring responsibility to the artist. The skilled player should no longer be an automaton. He should be a constructive artist, and, particularly in the national theatre, he and his fellows should constitute the body in which are lodged the artistic traditions of the institution. Every effort should be made to secure stability in the companies. The players must be bound together by something more than a commercial contract. Executive responsibility will be partly effective in securing solidarity; the position of the institution as head of the art will also have its force; and what pride does not accomplish may be further supported by the introduction of the pension system.

One further thing is forcibly brought to mind in the comparison of American stage conditions with those of Europe. It is the total lack of systematic training of the young player in all that pertains to the technique of his art. Aside from the efforts of two or three excellent private schools, the American player is left to the haphazard tuition of other actors and stage managers. They do differently abroad. It is demanded that the player at the national or city theatre shall be an educated man. For this reason many of the great theatres of Europe operate in connection with dramatic conservatories.

The necessity of some such trying ground and recruiting station for skilled young players is now one of the most serious of the problems of the practical art theatre. Lately word has come of the establishment of at least two such schools in Europe, and one or more are promised for America, established on broad principles. Just what relation such an institution should have with the hoped-for national or city theatre of America cannot now be said. Perhaps the theatre itself will grow out of the school, as the movement out of which the Chicago Drama Players developed was begun by a little nucleus of interested students, who studied under Donald Robertson in a dramatic school of Chicago. Perhaps the next endowed theatre will provide a conservatory as a necessary adjunct to its work, and will train the best students for places on the stage of the larger institution. The obligation of the institute of art to make way for the students of the art of the theatre has been recognized in the Carnegie Institute at Pittsburgh in a manner to give promise of even broader recognition in the future.

THEORIES OF REPERTORY

An endowed theatre cannot be judged by the character of any single production. In the same way that such a theatre must always stand for the perfection and balance of its *ensemble* acting, it must in the construction of its repertory strive for a balanced and representative ideal. Of all the problems facing such a theatre, the problem of the repertory is the one which is the most fraught with danger. And this problem has provided the greatest difficulties in the conduct of the subventioned theatres of Europe. No acceptable formula for the construction of a repertory has yet been suggested. The problem is one which varies with the traditions of the institution concerned, with the strength of the catalogue of available national plays, and with the peculiar demands of the era. In France, under the dominating power of the Comédie, the problem is reduced to the single question of the proper balance between ancient and modern plays. The traditions of the house are clear as to the quality and type of play to be accepted, and the drama of France is so rich in masterpieces that she need not look beyond her own borders. Until comparatively recent times, the main function of the Comédie Française has been to keep burning the flame of the classic drama of France. The prestige of the institution has gone far toward guaranteeing this. Matthew Arnold, in "The Literary Influence of Academies," has shown how substantial has been the influence exercised by formal standards in structure and style. To the French Academy and to the Comédie Française chiefly are to be credited that uniformity of style and dramatic norm which are characteristic of French plays. The Comédie Française will never give up its adherence to the traditions of the classics, for upon this rock it is built. Racine, Molière, and Musset still hold their place along with our more popular contemporaries. In times past the classics have had much the better of the argument, but in these days the claims of the moderns are pressing close and winning many battles. Against the dangers of too great exclusiveness, — for the doors of the Comédie are seldom opened for the foreign play, — the only corrective comes in the variety of types presented in any one week. In one of the forty weeks at this theatre, there may be presented, for instance, plays as diverse as "Les Précieuses Ridicules," "Ruy Blas," "Les Deux Orphelines," and "Le Duel."

The problem of the repertory in German theatres is different from that in the theatres of France. Instead of a dramatic tradition extending over three hundred years, Germany has a dramatic history of only one hundred and fifty years. Lessing, in the preface to the "Hamburg Dramaturgy," bears witness to the difficulty of finding good plays. "The choice of the play is no trifle, for choice presupposes quality, and if masterpieces should not always be performed it is easy to perceive where the fault lies." Partly through necessity, and largely, it must be admitted, through the natural receptiveness of the German temper, the doors of the great German theatres have been thrown open to the drama of Europe. German drama has thrived on the inspirations of neighboring nations. For many years Shakespeare has occupied a place of honor in the Berlin theatres. Byron's "Manfred" was first produced in Munich. Ibsen and Björnson were welcome in Germany before they were at home in the theatres of their own land. The result has been that while French drama has excelled in construction and finish, German drama has excelled in social significance and versatility. It is clear that Germany has made a virtue of a necessity.

An ideal theory of the repertory, constructed from the practice of the endowed theatres of France and Germany, would perhaps include four classes of plays:

First: The acknowledged classics. These may be limited to one nation or chosen from the masterpieces of several nations.

Second: Plays important in the history of a people and of the theatre. These may not be the masterpieces, but they represent the "high places" in dramatic literature and, as such, need to be kept alive. Examples of such plays are the romantic plays of Hugo and the elder Dumas of France; though not made for immortality, these plays are kept alive by main strength at the Comédie Française.

Third: Plays typical of the best movements of the contemporary art of the stage.

Fourth: Experimental plays, venturing into new *genres*, and representative of a new art. For such plays there is little room on the stage of a national theatre. Their place is rather on the stage of the experimental theatre.

The American repertory theatre can learn lessons from both France and Germany. From France it can learn the vigorous and conscious fostering of those memorable plays which, under the peculiar commercial systems of production, have been forgotten. Methods of production being what they are, the oblivion of popular forgetfulness can hardly be counted more an index of lack of worth than could the dust of Melos which hid so long the classic Venus. The director of the New Theatre stated that a classic play is one which, after a hundred years, is still alive and wel-

come to the public. This definition might be just in
France, where popular appreciation has been maintained more nearly at a pitch of proper judgment than
in America. It can hardly be considered just in
countries which, in matters of dramatic art, are governed by untutored and shifting popular standards.
Many great English plays are known only through the
libraries. Thankless as the task may be, it must be
the duty of a representative national theatre to search
out the great plays of the past and place them in the
position in which they belong as acted plays. Shakespeare will always be popular when he is well acted.
So also will Sheridan and Goldsmith, but there are
plays by Heywood, by Beaumont and Fletcher, by
Massinger and Etheridge and Wycherley and Con-
greve and Steele, that should not be forgotten on our
stage.

A parallel has been drawn between the conditions
of German drama of the eighteenth century and English drama to-day. Like Germany, we too can make
a virtue of a necessity and enrich our repertories with
the best from foreign lands. The English, like the German genius, is alert to a voice from beyond the borders.
There is no reason why we too should not have our
Molière and our Beaumarchais, our Calderon, our
Goldoni, and our Lessing, along with our Shakespeare
and Goldsmith and Pinero. To us all these are voices
speaking a language comprehensible and not too alien
for pleasure as well as instruction. For what the Eng-

lish stage needs is the broadening of its lines, not nationally but psychologically. It needs the recognition
that the art of drama is as varied in its interpretations
of life as the life that it treats; that it is not always
and everywhere a plaything; that it is a noble and
dignified art, which, while giving pleasure, may also
be studied. If, instead of going beyond the border for
the claptrap of German farce and French intrigue,
we should import the masterpieces of these peoples,
dramatic taste would be greatly improved in depth
and comprehensiveness.

THE NATIONAL THEATRE AS AN EDUCATIONAL FORCE

Writing his preface to the "Hamburg Dramaturgy,"
Lessing says, apropos of the easy judgments of the
work of the theatre: "Only every little criticaster
must not deem himself the public, and he, whose ex-
pectations have been disappointed, must make clear
to himself, in some degree, of what nature his expecta-
tions have been. For not every amateur is a connois-
seur. Not every one who can feel the beauties of one
drama, the correct play of one actor, can, on that account, estimate the value of all others. He has no taste
who has only a one-sided taste; but he is often the more
partisan. True taste is general; it spreads over beauties of every kind, and does not expect more enjoyment or delight from each than its nature can afford."

It is good that we can go back a hundred and fifty

years for this admirable statement of a modern need. For the better drama cannot be brought about by the activities of the artist alone. When it comes, it will come as much through the constructive and discriminating taste of the critic as through the efforts of the artist. Understanding of great art comes either through communion with the forms of that art, or through careful study of the criteria underlying its expression. Great art may have upon it the marks of inevitability, but that does not mean that it must be inevitably understood. Indeed, it is a mark of much great art that it remains a closed book until cultivation and instruction make its symbols clear. The ends of this cultivation and instruction it is the province of criticism to serve. Criticism has the double function of evaluating the art and educating the lover of art. While it is pointing out values, it is cultivating the perceptions of values. The place that criticism can play in support of the social art of drama is a large one. A widely diffused constructive art of criticism, an art that reaches all minds and states absolute values in terms of popular taste, is even more necessary in the case of drama than of other arts, for drama depends upon the suffrage of the many for its existence. Excellent pictures may come in answer to the elevated taste of the few. Excellent drama cannot come to stay until the taste of the many can support it.

A study of dramatic history shows how closely the expository art of criticism has worked hand in hand

with the theatre in formulating for popular judgment
the attainments in the art. We have seen that, when
the founders of the Hamburg Theatre launched their
experiment, they called to their aid a great critic. More
was accomplished for German drama by the fiery logic
of Lessing than by the bravest ventures of the experimenters. Dryden, the first of the English moderns,
introducing a new kind of play, defended it in trench-
ant criticism. The beginning of the era of modern
French drama with Molière and Racine was accompanied by the beginning of French dramatic criticism.
With the developing art, there came a criticism that
explained the art. The place of dramatic criticism has
always been high in France, because, there, criticism
has always been a scholarly and constructive thing.
Criticism served to place the refined and developed
art of the Comédie Française within reach of many
minds, and the gain was a reciprocal one. The work
of Weiss, Sarcey, Lemaître, Faguet, Doumic, has accompanied the work of the theatre, interpreting the
theatre to the people and preparing the people for
the theatre. Under such a conception as this, criticism becomes a high and necessary art, for it is an
art of arts, the maker of standards and the dissem-
inator of light. Lemaître, the brilliant young professor of rhetoric, who followed Weiss as critic of the
"Journal des Débats," reveals in his "Impressions" a
completed æsthetics of the modern stage. Sarcey so
much respected criticism that he declined all honors,

even to the cross of the Legion of Honor and election to the Academy, that he might hold himself free for the better pursuit of his calling.

These things are full of suggestion for us. With the collapse of the theatre in England, dramatic criticism also failed. The nineteenth century shows us only two examples of men of acknowledged standing in other arts who seriously took up dramatic criticism, Hazlitt and G. H. Lewes. We have had other excellent critics, but none who has raised the art of criticism to a constructive plane beside the arts and sciences. The art itself has been a haphazard thing; its codes have been unformulated by the artists; the public has been quite in the dark as to principles of judgment. When good plays have appeared, they have been isolated, because not clearly to be placed; bad plays have gone their way to oblivion, neither author nor public knowing for the breaking of what law they had been damned.

No art can succeed that is out of reach of the criteria of its patrons. A theatre that aims above the reach of its average patron must either struggle along, building a clientèle by the slow method of cultivation; or it must formally supply the critical interpretation of its own efforts. It is easy to imagine what the artist would say to this second proposition. He would prefer to have his art "speak for itself." This is undoubtedly just what the director of the New Theatre wished this theatre to do. Throughout his conduct of the house, Winthrop Ames' management was a model of poise and tact. He was silent when a word would have put the cavilers to rout. But it is seriously to be questioned whether art should be compelled to depend upon its own speech, where a wise and pointed word might save it from long waiting and misunderstanding. The purposes of a national theatre are not for those who run to read, and they should not be judged by the snap judgment that makes or mars the fortunes of commercial ventures. For such a theatre there is need of an authoritative mouthpiece to voice the purposes of the institution, to expound the principles upon which it is working, and to evaluate strictly the attainments of the theatre in the light of the highest principles of art.

The art of the theatre has changed radically in the last fifty years, and the rules of technique of the new drama are still to be written. Artists are still struggling for the ultimate in dramatic expression, through media of speech, and silence, and action that are still unfamiliar in their own hands. Naturalism has thrown away many of the easy conventions of the old stage, and now that naturalism is working its way into other forms of the symbolism of truth, artists are beginning to express themselves through finer filaments of communication than drama has been accustomed to use. Half of the meaning of a great modern play is in the unspoken and the unacted. It is in the "overtone," as they say of Ibsen's plays.

While these things are going on in the art of drama
and acting, audiences are continuing to learn their criteria of the stage from the popular successes of the
bright lights. What wonder that good plays mean to
them only something incomprehensible and annoying?

The new art should not have to wait until taste has
grown up to it. The endowed theatre will always be
as much a social institution as it is an institution of
art. It will owe it to the people as well as to the art
that the principles upon which its work is done shall
be laid open for those who will to read.

It is necessary that the national theatre should not
attempt more than it is fitted to do. Many dramatic
movements are at work in our social order and these
should not be confused. There are advanced theatre
movements, free theatres, experimental theatres, repertory theatres, and many other kinds of non-commer-
cial theatres. All these are valuable. But the national
theatre works on a definite set of principles of its own.
They are: that art is stable, that there are continuing
values in art, particularly within the limits of a nation
or a race, and that the rôle of the sedate art-lover is to
conserve that continuity. On this point we have lost
in England and America, not only because we have
hesitated to make experiments for the future, but
because we have cut ourselves off from the past. A
theatre cannot be considered a national theatre at its
best unless along with the impetus of the new it pays a

deserved tribute to the old. It is the function of the
state theatre to conserve the art resources of the nation.

In just what form the American national theatre
will come, no one can say. Our study will have been
for nothing if it has seemed to indicate that the forms
of the European theatre should be duplicated in
America. By imitating their form we can get nowhere.
The hardest lesson the New Theatre taught us was
that we cannot begin where France and Germany are
at present. Behind all the free theatres, the art theatres, and secessionist theatres of these countries lie
the abiding achievements of their national theatre,
a theatre which spells standards as well as opportunity for the younger worker, for it has supplied ready
to hand a body of critical opinion on matters of the
theatre. We have not this background, and for this
reason our work for the present must be more fundamental. To begin at the beginning requires patience
and modesty. But this we must do. We must follow
where the slow development of our institutions leads
us, into a national institution of the theatre which
is planted in our soil and nourished of our substance.
It may be that it will have no formal dependence
on the state. Perhaps it will be self-supporting. Or
it may be endowed by a far-sighted philanthropist.
One thing is certain. For the present big ambitions
must be forgotten. Let us not delude ourselves into
thinking we can leap to our station. Success in this

movement will come by means of many failures; and through the slow adjustment of many forces to a single end. The best sign of hope just now is the fact that social movements, once begun, do not stop half-way.

CHAPTER II

Is art its own justification and its own explanation? Or does it refer back to conditions behind itself for the sources and standards of its existence? No critic can altogether ignore these questions, for in the pursuit of his æsthetic judgments he sooner or later finds himself face to face with speculations that apply not only to his art but to the entirety of life. The further he goes in his questions the more likely he is to see that art is not a primary human activity, but a secondary activity, and that, as his judgments on art are refined and clarified, they tend to identify themselves with the judgments of those who think most clearly in matters of living. He ceases then to look for rules of art apart from rules of life, but tends rather to seek in life for the ultimate sanctions of art.

Now, there are many different kinds of art, and as they differ the form of their sanction will differ. Some, the making of gems, the carving of friezes, all the arts of detached ornament, may serve that strange and quite personal thing called "curiosity," the desire for an individual and satisfying beauty. But on the other extreme there are arts that seem to apply to man in his group relationships rather than in his individual yearnings, and to operate through organization rather than through individual vision. Such an art is architecture, and to this class also dramatic art belongs. And these arts we call social arts. But it needs to be remembered that in both cases the art seeks for, and finds, a sanction outside of itself in the life and spirit of man. The emphasis differs with the differing demands of the human spirit, whether of curious speculation or of mass consciousness. But there is no quarrel between the arts. There is rather a mutual serviceableness. The instinct for a curious beauty can on the one side be shown in the social art of drama, and on the other side the methods of organization can be brought to bear in the making of ornament. The boundary lines between the arts are fluid, and while each art keeps its function, it tends toward a universal expressiveness. Like the world of man the world of art is a single world.

What do we mean when we say drama is a highly socialized art? For an answer to this question we may well go back in thought to the early periods of community life, when there were developing two separate social activities. On the one side there was physical contest and sport, and on the other side religious festival and ritual. In the first of these there is expressed the earliest of man's ethical attitudes, as these are related with his leisure activities. In the second, we find the earliest application of æsthetics to social activities. These two activities appeal to different sides of human nature, present no less in civilized than in primitive man, and both of them provide strong factors in the constitution of the dramatic.

If we study these activities, we find that the first appeals through feats of strength and skill; the second appeals through the exercise and stimulation of the senses. In the case of feats of sport the pleasure secured to the onlooker is that vicarious pleasure which under society takes the place of individual participation. This pleasure is largely mental, sympathetic, and is essentially social in character. And likewise in the early ceremonial the purpose was to secure for the individual through the channels of society that stimulation of the senses that awakens to fuller and keener life.

It is clear that in both these activities the essential thing lies quite out of reach of any individual activity, and locked up in the fabric of common social experience. It is not until social function puts its stamp upon these activities that they take on any beyond the simplest and most rudimentary meanings. Then, however, as if inspired by a vibrant mass consciousness, a new social activity begins to develop, dedicated from its birth to the voicing of a peculiar message. Drama begins for society where speech begins for the individual, in the first rude attempts to give language to unspoken meanings.

Society is more than the sum of its individuals: so drama is more than the sum of individual messages.

For it is soon discovered that under the force of society there open up to view great orbits of truth never plumbed by the telescope of individuality. Growing with the growing complexity of the society from which it springs, and whose mouthpiece it is, drama develops to forms beyond anything promised in the earlier and simpler activities of individual life. From behind the service of praise to the victor, the ceremonials and liturgies over the dead, and the prayers to the gods, through the developing sense of beauty aroused by the harmonies of sound, the arrangements of line and color, and concordant posturings, there steal intimations of spiritual regions lying quite beyond the imagination of the artist of individual expressiveness. In this way society discovers itself when it discovers its drama.

A DEMOCRATIC ART

It has been said that drama is the most democratic of the arts; that it is in fact the only art which is essentially democratic in character. Is this the assertion of a partisan or can it be defended? If we study any one of the other arts, music, painting, sculpture, or poetry, we will see that there is in their substance and form of appeal no essential dependence on social groups. Apparently any one of these arts could exist, as far as content is concerned, in a quite unsocial world, and no one of them demands for its appreciation anything more than the alert sense of beauty in the individual. It is quite possible to conceive of the proper artistic response between a picture and a single individual seated alone in a museum of art. A piece of sculpture presents its beauty to the individual better than to the crowd. So also the æsthetic reaction secured from the playing of a sonata in a closed room by an isolated individual is as satisfactory and complete as that which comes to one member of a group. Poetry, too, is as truly poetry when read alone as when read aloud to a large body of people.

All these are arts which depend upon artistic criteria which may be as thoroughly developed in the individual as in society. They appeal directly to none of the essentially social functions. It is drama alone which, springing out of the social functions for its subject-matter, depends upon these functions for its understanding and is incomplete without them. Any one who has attended the last rehearsals of a play and has noticed how the lines and situations upon which the author has placed his best thought, and into which the manager and actor have thrown their most careful efforts, seem in the empty room to be flat and unprofitable, must have felt that something was lacking which could not be supplied by any individual, however skilled. And if, perhaps, he has attended the performance on a later evening when the audience chamber, empty before, is filled with intelligent humanity, and has noticed that the same lines and same situations are greeted with a clamor of approval, he has been led to appreciate how thoroughly drama is dependent on the crowd emotion. After this experience he may even feel himself justified in concluding that the one indispensable factor of drama is not author, or manager, or even player, but audience, and that the necessary characteristic of the audience is not so much either intellectual criticism, or favorable attitude, as it is simply that sense of mass coalescence that impels the audience to react as a social unit.

Now, that which is true of the appeal of drama is no less true of its substance. In respect of substance drama is a democratic art, for it derives its being from the recognized and interrelated functions of society. No other art equals the drama in sheer immediacy of method. No other art is so direct in uncovering the human purposes of men and women. Any comparison between one art and another upon the score of universality would lead one into unprofitable speculations. However, whether drama is more universal than other arts or not, — and certainly there is something that could be said in defense of this theory, — it cannot be questioned that it is more immediate and concrete. Drama is the art which most accepts the symbols of common experience, in which the simple formulas of everyday living are made, more than in any other art, to serve as the channels of spiritual expression. And it gains this immediacy at no expense of subtlety or depth, for it retains always the power of signifying by the most concrete means imaginative values of the greatest delicacy and remoteness.

Beyond this characteristic of concreteness in drama, which will always be the explanation of its great hold upon the people and its power as a social instrument, lies the fact that of all the arts drama is the only one in which the substance of the art is identical with the substance of the thing signified. The art of sculpture, taking stone and clay as the substance of the art, translates the rude outlines of these materials into forms indicative of the values of humanity and spirituality. Painting, acting under certain conventions of perspective, takes the substance of canvas and oils and water colors, and conveys through these the values of beauty. In the same way music restricts itself to the artificially created phenomena of sound, and secures from the combinations of sounds in harmony and discord symbols applicable to the farthest reaches of psychic meaning. In the case of all these arts the substance of the art is diverse from, and often apparently inconsistent with, the substance of the thing signified. As a result these arts require for their understanding an acceptance of conventions, some of which go very far into the regions of the complex and even of the artificial. An understanding of the art of music, even the enjoyment of the best music, is not an immediate power; it is a developed faculty of the mind and taste. So also of painting and sculpture. There is nothing immediate in the mind of man which provides criteria for the understanding of the greatest in these arts. For by the disparity of their substance from the substance of the thing signified, and by the impediments of convention and developed technique built up between the art and the natural understanding of man, these arts are necessarily appropriated to the enjoyment of the cultivated taste.

Compared with these arts, if we turn to drama, we see how complete is the identification of the substance of the art with the substance of the thing signified. Taking living men and women, with their words, their gestures, their peculiarities of speech, their expression of face and modulations of voice, their particularities of physical control, the drama identifies with these in direct and immediate order the symbols of its art. There is between the artist and his auditor no clash of uncorresponding symbols. Developed as is the technique of drama, its fundamental theories are most simple and immediate. The power which is thus given to drama as an organ of popular appeal is not given to any other art. It takes no high sense to appreciate the truth or the beauty of a play. In those cases in which the substance goes beyond the understanding of the auditor, the play may be beyond his reach, just as one man may fail to understand another man of profounder character, but there is nothing in the formulas of even the greatest plays that puts them out of the reach of the ordinary man. Euripides and Shakespeare, Schiller and Synge, have that largeness and at the same time simplicity which do not go beyond the understanding of the general.

Furthermore, as drama is the immediate art of social humanity, it necessarily includes and implies all other arts and social activities. In a definite sense it is the art of arts, just as it may be considered the art of social man. For if it is to be true to the essential nature of man, drama must do justice to all the factors and expressions of that nature. In these there will be included the stimulations rising from dancing, from design, from music, from religious and folk ceremonial. So also drama includes immediately all those factors which we have learned to consider essential to the understanding of the life of man. Not only the man himself, but the house in which he lives, nature as background and nature as environment, the atmosphere he breathes, the soil upon which he stands and to which he returns, being factors of life, are factors of the play. And these must be presented in their close relationship to the man, for in the truest sense they are part and substance of him. A man is more than his physical body. "I am a part of all that I have met," is a dictum that expresses a whole social philosophy. And beyond any other art drama presents the facilities for the treatment of man in this all-inclusive sense. Drama can present that subtle background making up the life of man, which is yet so indefinite and illusory that it well-nigh escapes statement. By the factors of its peculiar technique drama serves to express those activities of human life, most important as features of humanity, which lose their greatest verity when formulated under the symbols of other arts. On the one hand, drama includes and expresses the predicative values of life as they are involved in an alert human mind speculating upon its own processes, and at the other extreme it opens the door upon those intimate and delicate insights which are the peculiar intimations of the static arts of sculpture and painting.

We have said that the play lives upon the responsiveness of the people in social mass assembled. In a deeper sense the great play is not only dependent upon the people for life; it is the creation of the people. This, which is common enough in all the arts, is peculiarly true of the play. A great play is greater after fifty years than it is when the author writes, and the manager first produces, for in this time there has been added to the play a wealth of new and vital meaning. Each character and each symbol of the play has taken on, under the light of the particular civilization in which it is produced, connotations which are of the fibre of that civilization. Shakespeare's plays were at the time they were written distinctively plays of Elizabethan England, no less Elizabethan plays because they were so often concerned with alien topics. In the centuries which have followed their composition they have almost ceased to be Elizabethan plays.

But they have become even more English than they were at first through the gathering about them of the symbols of national consciousness. More than that, they have become also German plays in Germany as their symbols have been made to serve for the expression of Teutonic life, and French plays in France. And as time has gone on bringing new eras with their own formulas and social issues, these plays have become modern in the truest sense of the term, for successive societies have interpreted their symbols in terms of new meanings.

In one further and very important respect drama may be said to be a democratic art. We have shown that drama accompanies the growth of civic consciousness, that it becomes at first the play and amusement function of society, and that from this function, as society develops in psychic and æsthetic demands, there gradually develops the highest artistic expression in dramatic form. All along the progress of society, from the first rude relationship of men in the wilderness to the most refined communion in the Platonic city beautiful, drama accompanies and is involved in the progress of social institutions.

Now, it may be said that the progress of society is always in the direction of breaking down the impeding barriers between personality, and in coördinating individuals efficiently into the mass. The state in its best expression is achieving the change of men into Man. In the same way the art of drama is achieved.

make spiritual things flesh. And through the lips of his character Shakespeare lays down another specification for dramatic truth. It must deal not only with the "body," but with the "body of the time." In other words dramatic truth is always predicated on the age. It arises from fidelity to the eternal order of things expressed in terms of the particular and the temporal. If we are to discover what is dramatic truth for any age, we must discover the underlying characteristics which constitute the essence of the age.

An implication of this requirement is that, at the point at which dramatic art seizes the facts of life, these shall not have been formulated by history or scholarship. It is not with the dead and static facts of a formulated world that drama is concerned, but with the living facts of a world that is testing new values. It is the sign of the veritableness of a social fact that it is a changing and not a fixed thing. Society in every age is a matter of present evolving factors. So art likewise is concerned with the becoming rather than with the being; and more with that which is to be than with that which is. For it is the mark of the artist that he has an alert sense, that to him truth means values not yet formulated. Yeats has said, "Art is the sign of values not yet understood, of a coinage not yet minted." Another has said, "In art there are only revolutionists and plagiarists." It is the part of science and scholarship to be concerned with the past as it extends up to and explains the present. It is the part of creative art to be concerned with the present as it looks out upon and constructs the future. This, then, is the index of great art that, like the social movements of any period, it is prophetic of a coming order.

And Hamlet asked further that the player give the time its "form and pressure." Here is a thing differing from substance, and from modernity, and as important as either. For another art it would be perhaps "color" or "touch" or "style," but for drama this requirement is best expressed as "surface." This is no mere external requirement of finish in a play. It is of the fabric of its truth in that it has to do with the unit of society which it is the province of the artist to interpret in his work. It is impossible for the dramatist to take generalized human beings for his substance. He must take particular human beings as they are played upon by particular social conditions. For this purpose he can use only apprehensible social units which present surface characteristics and differentiated values.

The division of art among national and racial lines is no mere matter of patriotism. It goes back to the natures of men themselves, seeking their proper place upon the globe, experimenting for a relative social equilibrium, and struggling for a national speech. So far in world history the nation has been a means of human administration. It would not be too much to say that the best things in social life have been gained by means of the particularized social groups organized in races, and nations, and provinces. In art likewise national lines have been means of administration. Coherent social groups have served to increase rather than to lessen the power to express a universal message. It is probable that in the future as in the past, in spite of the efforts to federate the world, those dramas will be most universal which magnify humanity through the lens of national or provincial life. As an instrument of spiritual economy and concentration, it is improbable that the nation will lose its significance for art within the imagination of man.

Indeed, so far from broadening the outlines of social administration, the tendency in art has always been and is to seek out the smallest apprehensible unit of society which still presents in maturity the graces of unified social life. If we look over the history of art, we find that it is those nations which have been most clearly cut apart from their neighbors that have been the best breeding-grounds of art. They may have been cut off by natural divisions, and by the barriers of mountain or sea have been forced to find among themselves the materials of their destiny; or they may have been cut off by racial prejudice and strife, and have discovered themselves as a nation in fighting their foes. In either case it has been the clearly organized nation which has most early found speech. In like manner the speech of art has been found to come most readily to the smaller rather than to the larger units of race or nation. In many cases that which we know as the art of the nation is, as a matter of fact, the art of one of its provinces. And when this is true, it is usually the province which is drawn together by external or internal forces into the most dynamic social life that finds the earliest language in art. How much the art of the world is in truth the art of small and coherent provinces is perhaps not recognized until one studies the history of art in the light of social history.

This, then, is a requirement for truth in all art, and particularly in the drama, that it shall show the "form and pressure" of the life of which it is the outgrowth. Sometimes this is called "local color"; sometimes "national backgrounds." By whatever name it may be called, the thing itself is a verity that cannot be gainsaid when present, and cannot in any case be imitated. It is as much part and parcel of a great work of art as a peculiar flavor of speech is an attribute of a district. So far from limiting and curtailing free expression in a work of dramatic art, it is an instrument of peculiar richness and subtlety in discovering the deeper places in human experience. Without it a play is not completely a play in the same sense that a man without a country is not entirely a man.

We have found in Shakespeare's words, spoken through the lips of Hamlet, several tests by which we can judge the truth of a play in relation to the society which produces the play. Applying these tests, we see why so many plays fail. It must be apparent that any effort to maintain one standard of playwriting from age to age by fortifying the conventions of its technique, so far from serving the cause of truth is a fundamental pursuit of error. In the same way the effort to transplant to one nation the dramatic art of its neighbor is conducive to falsehood. Dramatic truth differs from generation to generation as the generations differ, and varies in manifestation from one nation to another. This is the most fundamental of all lessons, and yet the one which artists are most prone to forget: that one nation cannot express its social and spiritual values in terms of the art of another nation; that one time learns little in the statement of its inner meaning from the processes of speech of a preceding age. That dramatic art became a region of absurdities and falsehood is to be ascribed mainly to the ignoring of these truths.

And so it must be clear that, while dramatic truth is a certain thing, it is not an absolute thing; that while we cannot place our hands on any formula and say, "Here is the truth, and here, and here," there are yet ascertainable bases of truth that make it possible to say from what sources of human experience and principles of human expression it springs. So far we have been concerned merely with showing the need of a close relationship between dramatic art and the society of which it is an expression. But unfortunately there is no guaranty of perpetual values in this. Some periods are what are called transition times; in others the pendulum seems definitely to swing backward. The art which represents such an age may satisfy all the laws of its being and still be doomed to pass away with the diseased age of which it is the sickly flower. If we would look for the larger truth in art which will live from age to age, we must find not only a test of the art by the standards of the age, but a larger test by which the period and its art may be judged at once. And that test may itself be a social test.

Drama and the social order from which it springs must both be judged by their fidelity to the best principles of a never-expanding, self-perfecting social life. What are the tests of this? They are, first, for any movement or play, "Is it natural?" and second, "Is it socially constructive?" The requirement that at its heart drama shall be natural is equivalent to the requirement of sincerity that is laid upon all human works. But it is that fundamental sincerity that requires that the work shall be the result of a primary creative impulse, that it shall express by simple rather than perverted means the life that lies behind it. Above all, it is the requirement to be unaffectedly in accord with the eternal order of things. Art is not the voice of the anarch or the Anti-Christ.

But beyond this requirement of the natural there is one that springs more nearly from the social sources of our art. Individually man is disposed to concern himself with the present. It is when he becomes a social being that his activities broaden into the activities of preparation. In the extent to which they are socially minded men busy themselves with coming values. Society is always chiefly concerned with its future.

Here is another test of the larger truth in drama, that it shall be alert in the service of the coming prosperity. Drama shall not only be natural, but it shall itself be socially constructive. We have a right to demand of our drama that it shall conduce to upbuilding and social health. It is laid upon drama by the conditions of its substance that it shall promote that social solidarity of which it is itself the outgrowth and the completest expression in art. A play which by conception or influence is anti-social is an anomaly and a perversity.

We have here some larger tests of dramatic truth than those which have been given before, for by these we can learn not only whether a play is true according to the standard of its time, but whether it is true by the standard of all time. In order that a play may live it must be one with the expanding purposes of social progress. More than that, it must have served its part in clarifying social issues and in formulating a better order. By the use of these tests we get an abundant light on the fortunes of the plays of the past. We see why some plays, rapturously hailed by their contemporaries, passed away to early neglect. Perhaps they so emphasized the surface accidents of the time as to mistake the skin for the flesh, and the body for the soul, as did Ben Jonson, and so passed away because they were not natural. Or perhaps they spun a beautiful world of illusion out of the fabric of false sentiment and overblown passion, as did the Romanticists of France in the last century, and so passed away because they were socially destructive, as falsehood always is. By these tests we see, too, why some plays have grown into an ever-broadening prosperity. They may have emphasized the tragedy of life; they may have ridiculed its weaknesses and foibles; they may have been crowded with clowns and buffoons; they may have thrilled with a luscious line, or been touched by the pain of deep experience; they may have reflected but the passing joy of a day, and have passed away with the laughter they evoked; or they may have created for coming generations the ideal of a new and ordered cosmos; but whatever the purpose or the class to which each belonged, we may be sure that it was justified in its place according as it was natural and socially constructive.

By these tests we are helped to a better discrimination, and are led not to expect too much of particular plays. Some plays which can never be considered great are still to be vigorously defended as they satisfy a peculiar temporary requirement. Each age demands its language even though that language may not be the voice of beauty. More than that, in an art of the broad complexity and appeal of drama each class and critical school of society demands its own particular satisfaction. There is no æsthetic imperative in the art of drama to refuse these demands, nor can there ever be. The sooner we learn that all we can demand of dramatic art is that it shall satisfy those principles of social representativeness and constructiveness that have been suggested, the sooner we shall place drama on the high road to the attainment of the very highest things both as an art and as a social function. The hue and cry against the "morbid" play, against the motion-picture show, the vaudeville, and the melodrama, may do more harm than good in that they will turn back upon society those impulses which otherwise are finding a fairly normal, though perhaps unbeautiful, release.

Without defending the "morbid" play as an absolute thing, it may still be said that many a critic whose sensibilities are too tender to permit him the sight of blood condemns the true because it fails to foster his illusion of life. There are times when iconoclasm is the only true social constructiveness, and when health implies and requires the fearless probing of disease. Let each man interpret the health of the coming order in terms of clear sight and resolute thinking. The result, if he is a playwright, may not be a play that will live for all time, but it probably will serve as a useful document in the hands of his contemporaries for the reading of their book of life.

Many see the downfall of drama, and perhaps of society itself, in the present vogue of cheap entertainment. They should rather rejoice in the tremendous

outlet now being found for the leisure activities of
men, that through these activities drama is securing a
stirring-up of the soil around its roots that will result in fruit some time.

By some it may be thought that this definition of
dramatic truth leaves little room for the drama of
ornament, the masque, the *commedia del'arte*, for those
new schools of drama that are rising as a reaction
against the burden of thought in the theatre, and are
therefore making their appeal to a refined sense of
sight and a new and expert symbolism of the senses.
In a sense this may be true. We have never yet discovered a measure of values as apt and on the whole
as judicious as the standard of longevity. This standard is, for our mundane fashions, the nearest approach
we can make to the spiritual ideal of immortality.
The judgments of time may be false, but the judgments of a long time are likely to be true. And to
the absolute creations, the marbles of the Greeks, the
plays of Shakespeare, we give the judgment of time-
lessness. No art can or does live save as it is expressed
in abiding symbols. We would regret this the more
did we not recognize that the thing that is lost is the
temporal thing. We do not regret that the Greek and
the Egyptian dancer is lost, and that the Grecian urn
and the Egyptian relief have been retained. For in
losing the one we have lost all that is necessarily temporary and of the senses, and in retaining the other we
have retained all that is permanent. In other words,

it is possible to translate all art that is worthy of perpetuity into the symbols of perpetuity. And if this translation cannot be made, the art is by this fact cut off from the standards of the abiding.

Now, from all times the permanent symbols of dramatic art have been spiritual and social symbols, and plays have taken their place in the timeless judgment by the appeal they make to the universal soul of man. Some plays that possess these social symbols still fail of perpetuity because the symbols, being peculiar to the age, lose their force in later times. But no play has lived without them. They may have been rich with all the appeals to the senses, but these appeals declined and were lost. In some of the plays there was displayed the perfection of the artist's form and design, but standards of form are not permanent in drama in the sense that they are permanent in sculpture and architecture. The plays that satisfy the only test our wisdom can supply, whether of Sophocles, Shakespeare, or Molière, have remained for the light they throw on the life of man.

Is there, then, in drama no place for curious beauty? This does not by any means follow. For the search for curious beauty is itself but an expression of the inner soul of man. Man is not cut off from his fellows by his riper judgments, the more recondite demands of his spirit. He is rather the more closely united with all men. The two artists of the Middle Ages who are most remembered for their humanity are Benvenuto

Cellini and Leonardo da Vinci. One was a gem craftsman; the other had a mind "enigmatical beyond the usual measure of great men." It is through the symbols of his searching for beauty that man is remembered from age to age if so be that his searching is expressed in abiding forms. And dramatic art does not close the door to this search. It demands only the abiding symbol, the permanent substance. If the new dramatist would express but the satisfaction of the senses, if to him light means only a palpable medium for new effects, if color and design and shadow are but ornaments, then, indeed, he has chosen in the theatre the wrong medium by which to perpetuate his impression. He might better have chosen paint or clay, which always have the faculty of adding to the sensuous symbol a worth beyond their form and color. But if the new search is not to stop with the sensuous symbol, but is to go beyond to discover new mediums for the revelation of the eternal values of man, then, indeed, will the theatre be enriched by the new theories of plastic and sensuous production.

WHAT IS DRAMATIC TECHNIQUE?

This brings us to the matter of dramatic technique. It seems to be the habit of critics as well as those who practice the art to deny dramatic technique, and to hold that much talk about technique is simply an effort on the part of the knowing to mislead the ignorant, or of the ignorant to deceive themselves. To some extent the current distrust of technique is to be respected, as it reflects the healthy desire to avoid meaningless affectations.

But there is also the tendency to despise technique as a thing, which, if existent, is a matter of tricks and subtleties. So a playwright is referred to as a "mere technician," and by these words is placed only higher than the author of positively bad plays, though the fact that the term is used usually implies that the play was a success. Now, I believe that we can show that technique is not a thing to be despised, that it is in fact the gift that makes a playwright's work succeed by whatever means he may follow, and that the contempt for technique grows out of a misunderstanding of what dramatic technique really is.

For after all, what is technique? Is it not simply the method used by the skilled workman in doing his work when that work is a piece of individual creation? Technique is not mere journeyman craftsmanship. It is the expert manipulation of all the expedients of the art to the end of the completest expression of truth through a substantial medium. So far from being tricky and oversubtle, the first and greatest requirement of technique is directness and sincerity. He who attacks the technician is either demanding of an art that which does not belong to it, — the story of the painting, or the sermon of the play, — or he is mistaking the imitative processes of the journeyman for the constructive systems of the creator.

There are certain definite requirements for the technician which become clear to us in the light of the social explanation that has been made for drama. In the first place, the skilled technician knows the materials of his art. If he is a sculptor, he knows marble and bronze; if he is a painter, he knows colors. And if he is a dramatist, he knows men. These things he knows primarily and absolutely. In the second place, the technician is a trained observer. He has a true eye. He may not know human nature, or flowers or trees by the formulas which science uses, but he does know how to observe clearly and truly, and to transfer what he sees into the terms of his material. In other words, he has the gift of correspondences, so that he can project the truth that he has observed into the forms of his art.

Now, let us ask ourselves what would be his task were the substance of the thing seen of the same nature as his medium? Would not this greatly simplify his work in some directions, while even more greatly complicating it in other directions? This is the task of the dramatic craftsman. He must express in a human medium his observations of human beings. So he must be skilled as few are in human nature itself. His correspondences are, indeed, those subtle necessities which arise when the thing revealed must serve as its own expressive medium.

And if there has been any truth in the argument we have been making so far, we must believe that the dramatist must be a master of his age. He must be in fact a discoverer, for no mere acceptance of current formulas will keep him abreast of the age. He must divine and illuminate the implicit formula. The current formula is, by some strange paradox, always behind the time. By the necessities of his medium and of his substance the dramatist must be an independent thinker. Looking out over society he finds floating abroad conceptions that are not formulated in textbooks, or outlined in social codes, but are diffused through society, implicit in its processes, governing all it does. And these things that he finds in society it is his business to translate into the formulas of his art, that through it there may be turned to society a reflection of itself. With his art he creates a new world of dramatic correspondences. Not necessarily by taking thought, but by a creative divination the dramatist evaluates the characteristics of an age in terms of representation. His world of the stage is not identical with the world of reality, but parallels it and corresponds with it.

More than this, the true dramatic technician mirrors the soul of the age by presenting all of its complexities in ordered form. Bending upon the social world a discerning eye, he not only creates dramatic correspondences; he also draws together all the lines, focalizes the strains of force and tendency, converges currents that to the careless eye are vagrant and disconnected. He makes of his world of correspondences a true and yet an ordered thing, stamped with the evidences of nature's complexity, yet complete in itself, presenting some of life's mystery, yet so clear that he who runs may read. The implicit laws of social solidarity he makes explicit on the stage. In his way he is a distinct and valuable type of social servant, for he isolates the vague social ethics governing the time and in making it dramatic makes it dynamic.

Like substance like form is a law of art. And as the substance of drama, based upon the age which brings it forth, is ruled by a kind of slow-moving destiny, what more natural than that these same laws should be made to apply to the structure of the play as well? Naturalism grew out of the application to dramatic structure of those principles of economy, directness, and scientific efficiency that have been the governing principles of the age. And the new pictorial art of drama of Craig and Bakst and their followers, — it, too, is the outgrowth of the social background, of the sensitive soul of the artist wearied of the crowd and noise of the market-place, seeking in isolation and in quiet the rarer fruits of beauty. Naturalism was the outgrowth of a positivistic sociology. The new art of the stage is the outgrowth of individualism — the denial of the social bond for the sake of the more intense pursuit of the stimulation of the senses and the delights of play. In either case the inevitable laws of nature were at work to construct an art true to the fabric of the time in content and in form. And the play is but half understood when considered for itself alone.

In this sense the dramatic technician, though he may have no original message to propound, is serving to give expression to important truths. It may even be said that the more the dramatist is willing to sink his own creed and programme in the task of writing plays as well as he can, the more likely he is to perform a great task. In other words, it is the first business of the dramatist to be a good technician. Rather than emphasize the formal message of the great dramatists, we should say it is the most negligible element in their work. Ibsen's artistic life is absolutely consistent. But it is a consistency of growth and therefore of variety. His plays present, not the "message" sought for by hundreds of clubs, but a series of creative observations. Throughout his career he occupied one place, but he faced many ways, and the whole modern world came under his eye. And this is as it should be. Ibsen himself was first a dramatist, and his opinions grew out of the specific dramatic alignments in which he found himself successively interested. One would venture the assertion that he was really not a thinker at all, but the greatest stimulus to thinking our age has known. And if this may be said of Ibsen, it may be said in lesser degree of all other dramatists. They are creators and not theorists. They create in a world of the imagination an ordered, apprehensible fabric governed by the laws and

instinct with the spirit of the complex fabric of society
itself.

The dramatic technician is, therefore, both citizen
and artist, student of society and imaginative creator.
Good case could be made for the argument that the
dramatist led the sociologist in the discovery and
legible statement of the formulas of nineteenth-century social organization. Certainly, in the work of the
dramatists there is first reflected the change from the
age of enthusiastic faith and upbuilding to the age of
intellectual doubt and iconoclasm. They led the way
as theatrical purveyors who knew how to get theatrical
value out of contemporary life. Yet who would say
there was not social value in this technique? Dumas
in discovering the *demi-monde* provided a magnificent
expedient for dramatic clash. The value of this discovery transcends mere theatrical significance and
rises into the regions of social imagination. Isolating
for the sake of dramatic clearness a large social class,
Dumas also isolated this class in our social thinking.

The dictum, "What ye sow, that shall ye also
reap," taught long by revealed religion as an abstract
truth, adopted by Positivism as applicable to the social fabric no less than to the individual man, took on
vital social force when the modern dramatist discovered in it a late scientific correspondent of ancient
fate. True as it is in society, its operation ordinarily
extends over such long periods, and is diffused through
so many separate events, that its real force is lost

because its action cannot be followed. Here the dramatist steps in, and drawing together the lines of influence and action symbolizes in one small group a process that in society may be distributed over a community, and thus out of chaos there comes the truth, "Social character is social fate."

In the same sense the cult of individualism, which has been so strong during the last generation, has broken through many of the social, intellectual, and religious conventions of the past, in pursuing the end of a free and unrestricted life for the sake of the mere joy of living. Strangely enough, the note of freedom came into the substance of plays long before it appeared in the construction of the play itself. For freedom was, first of all, a conception, an ideal, and so it was accepted by the dramatist as an ideal to be formulated and fought for. What has been the result of this in society and how may it be stated? So confused is the social surface, so intricate are the lines of action and reaction, that it is difficult to draw out of society itself the lines which suggest the meaning of this cult in contemporary life. Here again is the opportunity of the theatrical craftsman, plotting his lines with intricate care, working to a centre in the following out of motives and their consequences, to picture to us the meaning in individual tragedy and social dissolution of the "live your life" cult that has been in the air.

And after the naturalist comes another dramatist, to whom freedom is no longer an ideal to aspire to, but an opportunity to be seized. In showing the love of color, the impressionableness, the joy in play, the desire of release from burdens of the later artists, he is reflecting the impulses of an era of faith after strenuous days. What may be in store for the new era in society and art is not now clear. After a time of questioning and anxious thought there is something of a turning to the frank acceptance of simple things; there is dependence upon the support of the unmotived and the spontaneous. The love of rich color, not as of the child but of the adult, the paprika appeal to the jaded sense, the simplicity and also the affectation of the antique, the learned artlessness, the love of the grotesque of those who have been reared on the regular and the reasonable — all these are present in the air of the period that follows naturalism. And in the rarefied air that follows the storm voices are raised in behalf of a new art. It is a new mood of man. And the artist is but discoverer of that which is. He but fills in the design that has been sketched by a larger hand. And his new design he calls his new technique. Will not it, too, be swept away by other social storms as society gathers itself together for another assault on the gates of the future?

APPLICATION

Our argument could not have been followed so far without the reader discerning that it has some particular destination. Certainly, in the case of an art as concrete as is drama there need be no apology for its application to concrete measures. A test of the sincerity of the play itself lies in its amenability to this kind of practical scrutiny. And so we need have no hesitation in asking the question, "What are the results of the application of the principles already laid down to the condition of the American theatre today?" We shall in the next chapter study somewhat closely the present condition of the theatre in America. There are, however, some general principles which seem to attach themselves to the argument we have been unfolding, and as these are not narrowly concerned with America, we may well outline them here.

We in England and America are just now learning again, what we had forgotten for two centuries, that the substance of our art shall be one with the substance of our society; that the motives of our art shall be the motives of our social life. This law has been observed with more or less closeness by Continental nations for a longer time. The extent to which they have excelled us dramatically may be gauged by their greater fidelity to this fundamental law. And today we are learning a harder lesson, that of a close application to truth, studiously if it is difficult; fearlessly if it is unwelcome. We have been prone to relieve our stage of the necessities of thought, on the one hand, and of plain speaking on difficult topics, on the other hand. But a new and more truthful era seems to be at hand. This is not entirely the result of the dramatist's initiative, though he has had his part in it. It has come from the fact that a code of more careful and honest thinking is generally being applied to the consideration of all matters of social import. The victory for honest thinking has not yet been won, but the early breastworks have been taken. It need hardly be said that with the collapse of the citadel of pampered social falsehood there will have been accomplished the great and indispensable, perhaps the last, measure in the liberation of a vigorous dramatic art.

But the movement is not a narrow one. All over the world a dramatic renascence is taking place, and this can but be an indication of social readjustments. The significance of these dramatic activities in these days, when the influence of the canons of logic brought down from the upper ranks in society seems to have served to kill imagination in the lower ranks, cannot be overestimated. As yet nothing has been provided to take the place of that which in another time was faith in the mysterious and unseen. And yet life is as vital and as interesting in our day as ever it was. We might say that never in history have the broad interests of participation in all the world's projects been distributed so broadly as they are to-day. Life itself is a thing of passionate interest to thousands to-day to whom new opportunities have taught new responsibilities. We are all busy trying to pull ourselves over the wall by our boot-straps. Certain as we are to disappointment in many of these efforts, the attempt itself, vigorous as it is, is good exercise, and is food for our souls. In such times as these the drama cannot be other than a necessary art to give expression to the concrete social imaginativeness of the age.

What is the lasting value which we are to get out of our times? How is the zeal and enthusiasm of material and social and industrial improvement to be transmuted into those spiritual terms which in all times are the only ones which endure? I think that the answer to these questions lies in art, and that the particular art for our times is the art of drama. If we ask why it is that in these days of tremendous improvement in all the facilities of living, we are nevertheless in many respects behind the standards of living of the past, we will find that with all our intellectual self-consciousness, we are still lacking that cohesive social consciousness which in times past found expression in spiritual adventures in the world of imagination, in the sailing of unknown seas, in the faith in fables and folk-lore and balladry, and in the worship of a God of mystery.

The reawakened interest in drama of these days signifies a timid demand on the part of our people for an expression of themselves in terms of the only metaphysical that they know; that is, the social metaphysical. Without knowing or recognizing the true meaning of what is going on, men are struggling for a language congruous to their new necessities. Its first syllables are vague and incoherent like those of children's speech. The important thing is that socially we are trying to speak, and we are striving for utterance in the form of that art which beyond all other arts gives chance for social expression.

All this indicates that for society a certain significant stage has been reached. This is a stage partly of reaction, partly of achievement and self-discovery. It is a reaction from the destructive and skeptical tendencies of a period which was so much convinced of the falsity of the systems of the past that it had no eye for the promise of the future. To-day we are very much concerned with the future. The coming day represents, as well as anything can, in the eyes of people in general, the standard of the ideal, and the power of mystery. These things must speak through our art. Never, perhaps, with the blind and childlike unconsciousness of faith will we again undertake the building of our epos. It will now come as the conscious and assured creation of a mature society in which belief is not an offering from the gods to be accepted without question, but a truth to be seized and weighed. The beauty of the new art will not be the beauty of the wonder of the unknown, but of the wonder of the known.

CHAPTER III

ONE thing is soon discovered when we begin to study the present situation of dramatic art in America, and that is that its problems and most interesting developments are by no means limited to the theatre. It will probably be found, when the history of present movements is written, that the most important developments took place outside of the theatre altogether, in a society that had suddenly become acutely conscious of the necessity of exercise, and was turning to the drama as the most available of the arts upon which its forces could be spent and by which its leisure could be enriched. Largely as a result of this interest on the part of people in general, the present is an era of rapid and radical change in the theatre, and the theatre itself, as an institution, has been the centre of a hue and cry of random and irrational attack.

A calmer judgment will show that it is not in this spirit that better things will come. The best thing that can be accomplished by the present unrest is to direct attention to the abuses. The public cannot directly reconstruct the theatre; that will be the work of experts who will work under the force of public opinion. Inexpert criticism is almost certain to be superficial and destructive. Such criticism is prone to attack as the cause of a debased state of dramatic art instruments that are only factors in it, and to demand the abolishment of some of the most useful institutions of the stage. A judicious mind can see that even the weakest features of present theatrical organization are serving some good purpose, and that we have nothing to hope for from a blind and hasty revolution in dramatic procedure. Not seldom it happens that the things that are prophesied for a distant future by the visionary are taking place as a fact in the hands of the workmen of the present.

One thing that is particularly blamed in some circles is what is called "professionalism." The "profession" of the theatre has been blamed for its low ideals, its pandering to the crowd, its conservatism in the face of demand for change. These charges are unjust. There need be no fear of professionalism in the mind of one who studies the way things have come to pass in dramatic art. Professionalism is in fact an expedient by which the business of the theatre has been carried on. Some such practical expedient is particularly necessary in these days of widening contacts between the art of the stage and the people. If stage professionalism has been subject to abuses, these have been no more serious than the abuses that spring up in connection with other highly specialized activities, such as teaching and preaching, for instance.

It seems to me that a fair statement of the debt the

world owes to its professionals of the stage should in justice be made. At the start there is necessary a restatement of the standards by which the so-called "professional" and "amateur" spirits are judged. In many quarters it seems to be presumed that there is some essential divergence of ideal between these. Each looks upon the other with suspicion or contempt, the professional supposing the amateur is a mere pretender, the amateur easily assuming that the professional prostitutes his art for money. Both of these views are false and unreasonable. Moreover, they are mutually destructive. By any fair judgment the professional and the amateur represent two coöperative and sympathetic pursuits of the same end. No art can exist in health without at the same time a vital spirit of professionalism to supply the sinews, and a hearty spirit of the amateur to supply the spiritual support. It is a mark of the ill-health of drama for a century or more that the functions of both of these classes have been misunderstood.

To ascribe to the professional a selfish spirit is on the one hand as unjust, as on the other it is to accuse the amateur of being a dilettante and a pretender. To the amateurs of the arts we owe all that support that comes from the unconscious surrender to an art that one cannot practice. Art is always carried high in the affections of its amateurs. It is a mistake to presume that the amateur may not be well informed in his art, that he may not even now and then practice it acceptably. Through his peculiar interest in his art his taste is freed from many of the considerations that fret the practicing artist. What the amateur may mean to an art is revealed when we notice that when an art is vigorous and healthy it has the hearty support of a strong amateur spirit. All great artistic work, in so far as it has any outer stimulus, is done for the sake of the amateurs of that art. It is they only who can repay in discrimination and sympathy the careful toil of the artist.

But does not the very defense we make of the amateur indicate that his is not the primary position? Strangely enough, it is not to-day the amateur who needs defense. In reacting from the rigors of professionalism we have assumed that to the amateur belonged all the merit, and the professional has borne the brunt of blame for conditions that are not of his making. What is it we owe to him? In my opinion we are obliged to him for the existence of the theatre to-day with such glories as still attach to it. He it is who provides that skilled and technical mastery of the arts from which come our stable standards. He has supported his art in fair days and foul. The amateur deserts in time of decline. It is the professional, too, who creates for art the traditions that are handed down from age to age. And erecting these traditions into institutions he supports them and battles for them. He is the conservating force in art. The stage has most reason to be grateful to its professionals, for of all the arts the stage most works with shifting materials. In times that are impatient of restraint, ready always to identify the better with the newer thing, and the best with the iconoclastic, the professionalism of the stage has been the one bulwark of a conservative art.

So while the professional spirit may be accused of magnifying form at the expense of spirit, and of clinging to the old because it is the tried, it was this spirit that kept the stage alive through bitter days. By it such results as were accomplished were secured. And when society had so far found itself as to enforce a better dramatic expression, this, too, was secured largely through the coöperation of professional writers, actors, and managers.

Professionalism, therefore, while not perfect, is a characteristic instrument of present-day society in its relation with dramatic art. Such faults as it has it possesses in common with all the machines of man's social life, which operate by the counsel of compromise rather than perfection. A similar but not quite as strong a case can be made for Commercialism, which is sometimes identified with Professionalism. But commercialism is quite another thing. At the outset we must admit that the commercial principle practically represents society's ways of getting things done in these days. It is the system by which support is secured for all good things that are not matters of state grant or private benevolence. The sincere artlover has not yet come to the point — in America, at least — at which he can look with contentment on the prospect of either one of these latter undertaking the support of his art. And this hesitation to place art in the hands of the state or of charity is at bottom a healthy thing. It indicates the demand that democracy itself shall show itself to be worthy before it is endowed with the highest responsibilities, and also, perhaps, the feeling that the real utilitarian value of drama is a thing that is not to be ignored. This waiting spirit has compelled in the case of music and painting a kind of modified commercialism which is at best a compromise, and it has pressed the theatre over completely into the commercial market-place. And to many of the features of this state of the art no friend of the drama can be reconciled. Let us see whether some of the worst features of this system are necessary, whether, indeed, such commercialism as we have in the theatre to-day is an enlightened commercialism.

Granting that commercialism is good in its place, that according to the economic system of our time it may be necessary to compel art to adapt to a commercial régime, what is the chief case against commercialism in the theatre? Simply this, that, whereas the commercial system of the theatre was invented as a means of support of the drama, it has changed places, and the drama has been compelled to support the system. In truth, this may be the chief indictment of commercialism the world over, that what was contrived as a means of the securing of life has come to subsist upon life. This charge is particularly heavy in the case of the arts. While labor may live for a time chained to the car of money, art enchained dies immediately.

No one will deny that the first application of the modern commercial system to the stage was a benefit. In perfecting the organization of the theatre, in freeing the author and player from penury, it raised the theatre to the plane of a self-respecting profession. But it did not stop there. It was learned that what had been a precarious trade of half-vagabondish players could under organization be magnified to a tremendous business of purveying entertainment to the appetites of newly awakened millions. Long ago all purpose was forgotten other than the capitalizing of entertainment and art in the same way as transportation and oil are capitalized. The result has been deep-seated both as to society and art.

The commercial system has many things to answer for, but they are not the things for which it is generally called to account. For one thing its crimes are not so simple as those which have been charged to it. They are more insidious, not so concrete, and by no means so easily remedied. In naming the sins of the commercial system the stock catalogue is, the long-run system, the collapse of the stock company, the star system, the type system of acting. To tell the truth, these are not unmixed evils. Furthermore, they are more products of the new social arrangements

of our time than of any system of management, and
as such are to be defended rather than decried. In the
day of rapid transportation, of easy communication,
of general education, and of a universal demand for
centralization and economy, these things would have
followed in any case. No one would return to the old
stock system if he could, and the " long run " is now
and always was a matter of supply and demand. If a
thing is good there is every reason why as many as
possible should see it. Nothing would be gained by
attacking the " long run " as such; the conditions that
entail it should be changed.

The commercial system has more to answer for
than this. Its chief sin is that it has transformed the
theatre into an institution of fictitious values. The
specifications of this are many and explicit. They
have to do with the effect upon the theatre itself as an
institution, and also that negative effect which follows
in a society which has no sane and healthy outlet for
the activities of its leisure. Naturally, the first of
these, being more specific, will more repay study. The
second must be taken on trust, but its significance can
be read in more than one social record.

Let us see how it is that the commercial system has
made of the theatre an institution of fictitious values.
Chiefly this has been done through the emphasis that
has been laid on the commodity attributes of the
theatre. To-day the chief energy of the theatre is de-
voted to the selling of the wares. And all the allure-

ments of merchandising are used to stimulate trade. The result of this has been to set upon art a commercial standard that does not belong to it and that it can ill afford to carry. There follows an attempted marriage between art and business which always results in the subjugation of the more delicate party to the contract. The fictitious standards which are compelled by the commercial system have their influence everywhere. They have introduced a new standard by which a play is to be judged, the standard of "expense." Of course, it is far easier to judge a play by the money that has been spent upon it than by the other more indefinable standards. In this way attention has been directed to those things which are the mere appurtenances of drama, the facilities, the buildings, the dressing, and the expensive production. It is safe to say that a large portion of what is now spent in the production of plays is spent on something other than the real and veritable art itself, that the expenditure is really an expenditure in non-essentials.

This fictitious standard of expense is first seen in the theatre building itself. It is now necessary that our theatres shall occupy as nearly as possible the central portion of the town; that they shall be accessible from all parts of the city; and that a plant that is used only a few hours during the day shall pay dividends upon a real estate and building investment which in other businesses would be supported through the income of all the daylight hours. It was not so in the days of the giants. Then, when business was subordinated to the social or the art function, people went to their theatres rather than waited until their theatres lured them. The amphitheatres of Greece and Rome were sometimes outside the city. Shakespeare's plays were presented outside the city on the banks of the river Thames. But not to depend upon support from the past the example of the amusement park and the baseball pavilion prove that there is no need for a centrally located plant. The logic of the situation in our cities is all against crowding all the theatres into one restricted and expensive theatre district. If the theatre were not dependent upon fictitious values a theatre building could serve the neighborhood instead of the municipality. Indeed, the movement for outlying theatres is strongly on the way.

In advertising, too, we find revealed the fictitious character of present dramatic production. In the development of paid advertising for the exploiting of the business of the theatre, and in its twin-sister, press-agent puffery, we have the most efficient means of spreading through society those artificial values upon which the business of the theatre has lately existed. In the mystery thrown about the private lives of artists, the inflated popular estimates of the money value of acting and playmaking, in the false standards of expense applied to details in production and scenery, we have abundant witness that while the business of the theatre expands the art declines.

We are by no means contending against the self-support of the drama. On the contrary, we believe thoroughly that drama should be self-supporting, and that it could be self-supporting through all its grades from lowest to highest in any system in which the income of the theatre went back into its support. It is the artificiality of the system against which we write; its compelling of the art to carry the trade, rather than the trade to carry the art. There is no good and necessary thing that cannot be freely and independently self-supporting if its organization is so directed. The Church can hardly be called a charity. It is a self-supporting organization that pays its way and gives value received. But what happens when religion is capitalized for the sake of profit? Countless examples have shown that there is erected a tremendous capitalized institution, but that the Church of souls decays. That spiritual death that comes to commercialized religion comes likewise to a commercialized art, and for the same reason. Let us not suppose that art cannot support itself. Even the higher forms of dramatic art will secure a sufficient support when they are relieved of the weight of inordinate tribute to business, and are presented before men and women in no fictitious guise.

If we study in some detail the present condition of the stage in America we may see in what way the argument we have been developing works out in practice. Surveying the whole field of dramatic entertainment we find, as we would expect, that drama is organized all up and down the line to serve the different classes of intelligence and taste represented in the community. Naturally, the theatre is most active at points of the most widely distributed appeal. But strange to say, this is not the point at which it is most highly organized, or at which it pays the largest tribute. Taking the situation by and large, the heaviest organization and the highest "overhead expense" are found in the case of the so-called "legitimate" drama, or the drama of narrowest popular appeal. It is here that the faults of organization and commercial management are most glaring both in their business and art aspects. And this type of play is compelled to bear the largest burden of fictitious values, and to pay dividends that are not returned to the art side of the business.

Let us look at three types of dramatic entertainment, representing three orders of appeal, and varied systems of management. The first of these is the motion-picture theatre. Of all forms of theatric entertainment this has by all means the broadest social bottom. In ten years the motion picture has practically displaced many of the older forms of entertainment, notably the cheap melodrama, and has made precarious the situation of musical comedy. Now, the writer is by no means of those who consider the motion-picture show an unmixed blessing. There is every reason to hope that within a few years this form of entertainment may either be discarded for another of higher type, or that of itself it may evolve into something better. But for the present it must be said that the motion-picture entertainment is the one form of public amusement whose growth has been absolutely natural and unstimulated. Without aid from advertising, or the campaigning of business organization, it sprang up within ten years in answer to an unquestioned social demand. Recruited first from the audiences belonging to other types of entertainment, it soon began to create a new audience both in villages and cities. The daily audience of the motion-picture show is now throughout the country at least ten million. In other words every day one tenth of our population is to be found in the motion-picture show hall. Its patronage is now six times as large as the daily audiences of all other kinds of entertainment combined. It is largely a family audience and is recruited from the community. To-day there are fifteen thousand theatres of this type in the country, and this may be increased to twenty thousand before the end of another year.

The importance of this lies in the fact that it was the result of natural and popular growth. There was no fictitious allurement to mislead or compel. No form of entertainment has arisen in years that so thoroughly represents what the great mass of people want as does the motion-picture show. It came just in time to serve as an outlet for a restless and overcrowded urban life. And so far the organization of the motion-picture theatre has been of that type that involves fewest steps and least handling between maker and consumer. The overhead charges are low, the purely fancy expenses are practically none. As far as the people of the town are concerned, the theatre is a local institution. No one can feel that an unreasonable amount of his five or ten cents is sent away to serve some purpose that is not represented in the production itself. It is true that in recent years big business has taken over the motion-picture field, and has begun to exploit it by all the well-known methods of trade. To the extent that this is the case the motion-picture business has already begun to show signs of ill-health. An artificially stimulated taste inevitably flags, and witness to this process is not wanting in the field of the motion picture.

Perhaps the motion-picture entertainment will be of short duration. Such a question enters the field of profitless speculation. Certainly, there are some considerations that point to the fear that it may not always serve the natural social function that it has served from the first. By its very cheapness it is creating an entertainment habit among people. Particularly in the village the tendency is to exchange the spontaneous games of the green and the meadow for the less healthy interests of the closed room. On the side of social solidarity the motion picture suffers in comparison with the other arts of the theatre. In particular it lacks the human and social appeal. In all other forms of dramatic art there has been shown a hearty sense of participation between players and audience. No such reaction is possible in the case of the moving-picture show. The sense of mass in the audience is never appealed to. No other aggregation of people remains so thoroughly unamalgamated as the audience in a moving-picture room. From these points of view the motion-picture entertainment hardly satisfies the requirements of naturalness and social constructiveness that were laid down in the preceding chapter. But when all has been said, it still remains that the motion-picture show represents a veritable expression of present-day society and is within its scope serving a useful social function.

Doctrinaires are often pursued by the fear that lower forms of art enter into competition with higher forms of art and drive them from the field. That is not the case if both have a fair field, and if the higher art is not compelled to carry a handicap. Given natural processes all along the line, each form can prosper within its field. Naturally, the lower type of art makes more noise and is more distributed, because there are more people who want it. But as well expect the wealthy to discard the finer cloths because calico is cheaper, as to expect the cultivated and intelligent to select the lower art because it is the more popular. In both cases the decision is made by reference only to availability and the quality of the wares. If anything is needed to convince one of the truth of this, a study of the situation of the vaudeville show in comparison with the motion-picture show will be sufficient evidence. Of all the forms that one would expect to be seriously hurt by the motion picture, the vaudeville or variety theatre would be the first. We would perhaps grant that the variety show is higher in quality than the motion-picture show. Certainly, it is the form that most competes in type of appeal and interest, and it appeals generally to patrons of about the same order. Yet during the period of growth of the motion-picture show the vaudeville theatre has had the greatest expanse in its career. Vaudeville theatres have multiplied only less rapidly than the smaller picture theatres. More than that, during this period greater strides have been made in raising the standards of variety entertainment than ever before. The growth cannot be ascribed entirely to the growth of the entertainment habit. According to the principle of the destructive competition of the lower, this would have been satisfied by the motion-picture theatre.

The answer to this question goes back to the attitude taken by variety managers, and the system of organization provided for the accomplishment of their work. It was the managers of the variety theatres who first learned how to eliminate the fictitious factors from the business of the theatre, and made it, as nearly as may be in a selfish world, a system of purveying to an entertainment-seeking crowd by giving the crowd what it had a right to demand under the better interpretation of this order of amusement. It was the vaudeville manager who first broke away from the crowded theatre district in the central part of his city and placed his theatre on a side street and in the suburbs of the city. By so doing he brought his theatre nearer to his clientèle by encouraging the neighborhood theatre, a natural institution in itself. Involved in this was the release from the necessity of high expense in advertising. The average vaudeville theatre does not spend anything like the money on advertising that the legitimate theatre spends. In the matter of prices it has been the policy of the managers to keep the admission fees as low as possible. And they try to give as much as possible for the money. When necessary in order to lower the price, they shorten the programme and win by a rapid turning over of the wares. Most significant of all it has been the policy of these managers continually to improve the programme. And this has been done in no idealistic vein, but according to the dictates of an alert business sense, that has encouraged them always to be on the lookout for the new thing, and continually to try to keep abreast of improving standards of taste among the audiences. To-day the people are crowding the vaudeville theatres to see at least a dozen excellent players of first rank whom a short-sighted business policy has driven from the legitimate stage. This will hardly indicate that the people will not support high art of the theatre. They will support it when it is conducted according to sane principles of business, and they will not be diverted from support on account of the slightly lower caste of the variety theatre.

The influx of some of the best actors of the legitimate stage into vaudeville has a real significance. It signifies their flight from an ill-managed to a well-managed corps of theatres. It means the overflow from a legitimate theatre which a false business system has overrun with stars into a theatre with a broader social bottom. Then, too, there are some respects in which the vaudeville theatre offers to the sincere artist of the stage better opportunity for the pursuit of his own ideals of dramatic art. For one thing, it can and must tell simple stories. The demand to "fill the evening" at whatever expense of padding and irrelevancy that is forced on the legitimate stage is replaced by the demand for an action that is quick and to the point. On the side of artistry, where the vaudeville theatre touches art at all, it is not unlikely to give an encouraging reception to the genuine, the simple, and the good-natured. Here is no room for the falsehood of sentiment or of intellectualism. And in encouraging the one-act play the vaudeville theatre has been fortunately in accord with the trend of events in dramatic writing.

In one further respect of organization the vaudeville theatre is more fortunate than the organization of the legitimate theatre. This is in respect of the smaller units upon which its circuits are maintained. Unlike the legitimate theatre, which is controlled altogether from the distant centre of New York, the vaudeville theatre is administered in a series of provinces all of which look to New York, it is true, but each of which is independent in its field. It has been upon this provincial system that the vaudeville theatre has come to its highest efficiency. From San Francisco, Denver, and Chicago have radiated circuits which have done much to create an organization close to the social heart of the province. In this respect of serving an apprehensible social unit the vaudeville theatre has been administratively in advance of its more aristocratic colleague.

If we apply to the vaudeville theatre the tests of naturalness and social constructiveness that have been suggested, we see features a-plenty in which its productions do not satisfy the test. But the important thing is that it is on the high road, that its organization is sufficiently veracious and well founded to permit it to go straight forward to better things. And the managers and actors are discovering for themselves that some of the old features of the varieties must be eliminated in favor of other and more healthful forms of entertainment. As we showed in a former chapter, the whole progress of drama has been away from the purely individualistic, in which it is concerned with feats of personal strength and skill, toward the higher activities that are born of a conscious social life. It was with the individualistic, or at least unsocial, activities that the varieties were first concerned. The animal show and the feats of athletic and gymnastic strength and prowess served as the centre around which the vaudeville revolved, and these are quite lacking in appeal to the social sense. A careful study on the part of managers of the demands of the crowd has taught them that to-day the appeal of these unsocial entertainments is certainly diminishing. They are taking every year relatively a smaller place in the variety programme, and their place is being taken by the more highly socialized amusements. The tendency on the part of performers in these acts, crude as it is, to protect their act by an appeal to the comic sense is but in itself a recognition of the unconscious demand of the audience that the entertainment shall have some social basis.

In respect of a due regard for the principles of social constructiveness, it may be said that of all forms of theatrical entertainment, the only ones which formally undertake to protect the standards of social health are those forms which lie at the foot of the column. In the acceptance by the motion-picture producers of a workable system of moral censorship, and in the promulgation by the vaudeville managers of rigid rules in matters of morals and good taste, there is revealed an enlightened common sense that for some reason has not been characteristic of the business management of the legitimate type of entertainment. One need not be accused of defending the vaudeville theatre as a temple of art if he says that it is, in view of its function, the best organization of the theatre in America to-day, and that, as a model of making the system support the play rather than compelling the play to support an expensive system, it may be held up for the emulation of those theatre managers who deal with the higher class of art.

And now we come to the legitimate theatre so called. Enough has been said to show the writer's opinion that the organization of the theatre at its highest point is unnatural, artificial, and expensive. By building up fictitious standards it has all but alienated or completely destroyed the audience for the higher art of drama, and has gone far toward destroying the art of acting and perverting the springs of playmaking. In a discussion of this kind it is desirable to emphasize as much as possible the social and organization aspects, and permit the implications of art to take care of themselves. But there are sufficient indictments to be brought against the commercial system on the score of its social and administrative inefficiency.

Little need be said here about the syndicate system of theatrical production. Like professionalism, the syndicate is a bogey which is held up to the horror of the innocent. Within limits the syndicate system was a necessary outgrowth of the spirit and methods of the times. It was necessary and within reason for the theatre to make that use of increased transportation and communication facilities that other organizations are using to the end of greater efficiency. It was when the theory of monopoly and absentee managerial control entered that the harm was done, for with this system the manager lost all concern with his demesne other than the requirement that it return him his profit in as quick order as possible, without regard to permanency or health of the producing medium.

The system of organization fostered by this type of heavy centralization organized the entire country as tributary to one city. Every legitimate theatre in every provincial city was compelled to pay its tribute to the central power in New York. The result of this on the side of organization has been appalling. In the space of fifteen years the provincial theatres have deteriorated from local amusement enterprises serving the community that fosters them to helpless creatures of a distant master. The inevitable came quickly and with telling force. As the theatre was organized out of touch with its "apprehensible social units," it soon ceased to serve these units intelligently. The patronage, served fitfully by an intelligence hundreds of miles away, dwindled in character and amount. The cry went up that there is no support for the higher types of amusement, and the process of stimulating by artificial means an already alienated and perverted public taste went on. It is clear enough that neither malice nor cupidity need be charged against any one.

The system was an impossible one from the start, and every effort to bolster it up carried it further into the irremediable. There began that process which we now call the "collapse of the one-night stand," a deterioration tragical in the social history of our small towns and fatal to the sinew of our drama.

But while the life was being drawn from the provinces, it must not be supposed that the system was at first a financial failure. It might have been better if it had been, for then the eyes of those in authority might have been opened. Blinded to the truth by the flow of money from the outlands, they began to build castles and pleasure houses at home. The millions of tribute drawn from the circumference poured like a golden stream to the centre. From nowhere came the intimation that in killing such an impalpable thing as art the business itself might suffer. And so there began the era of theatre building in New York, theatre after theatre built out of the booking money and percentage tribute of the provinces. Later the same process was begun in the motion-picture field. The business of public amusement was organized to draw water eternally from a lake that is fed only by its natural springs. When the drain becomes too great the lake dries up.

Then the fictitious values upon which the theatre had been fattening began in their turn to claim their inevitable compensation. The public had been restive; its tastes had become unusually fickle; never before had it been so difficult to say just what the "public wants." But the true significance of this was not read first in terms of a diseased public taste, perverted and made irritable by years of bad feeding. Only a few theorists of the theatre saw this. The significance of these facts burst upon the minds of those in control when it was seen that the business of the theatre, always as uncertain as a young man's thoughts, had now become a greater gamble than before, with the odds against the house. But while the stream kept up, though in diminishing amounts, the building went on. Until suddenly there came a check, and from a most peculiar cause, a cause of such irony, that good old Davy Garrick, that artist-business-man of the theatre, might well come back just to smile at it. It did not come from the people; they could not help themselves. Nor did it come from the actors, though as a class they had come to recognize that never, even in the old days, had their positions been so untenable, their art provided so little recompense. It came from the authors themselves. In a day when to be a dramatic author is to have struck a Texas oil well, the cry went up, "We cannot get plays." And a dozen New York theatres opened to Shakespeare played by a dress-suit star and a press-agent-created *ingénue*. And in Youngstown and Medicine Hat the main theatre was dark, while Bernhardt and Bertha Kalich played to crowded houses in vaudeville, and Mrs. Fiske appeared in the movies.

This hardly seems the place at which one can review the influence this system of organization has had upon the play itself. It is when we see fictitious standards working at the heart of drama that the monstrousness of the indictment stands revealed. For the true values of art at the point where art needs to be most modest and retiring have been prostituted to selling the goods. The demand for truth which compels the dramatist to delve into secret and solemn places has been perverted into a pander to an unnatural taste for lubricity. The serious study of the problems of virtue and vice has become a morbid appeal to emotions which are not self-corrective. The faithful treatment of emotion has become a wash of sentiment for the tears of the crowd. The keen appeal to the sense of comedy becomes a sop to crude laughter. Even the intellectual idea which the world is discussing is stripped of its vitality, retains of itself only a semblance sufficient to sell, and is retailed in the form of dramatic platitudes. In other words, the processes, which within their class we found to be always working upward in the motion-picture show and in vaudeville, have here reversed their direction, and now inevitably settle downward. The theatre which should be natural and socially constructive becomes unnatural and socially disintegrating.

Now, one cannot admit that the sins of this upper institution of drama should be visited upon society. If an institution is not serving society, society sooner or later repudiates the institution. Nor are business methods to blame. It is the mistaken system of business that looks upon the art of the theatre as tributary to the bank-balance of a speculator. And there is no real lack of potential support. Dramatic art that can support itself at the bottom of the ladder can support itself at the top. There is not demanded the idealism of the artist, the sacrifice of the reformer, the charity of the philanthropist. These could be had in any event. What is wanted is that sane business acumen that knows the art of the theatre on its highest side, and knows how this may be supported as a business.

If my argument has been followed, it will not seem that the situation is hopeless. While our Jeremiahs are lamenting, natural forces in the hands of a few keen-sighted men are active in remedying things. And there are several signs that a new order of business management of the theatre is on the way. Partly this will come because men of the theatre are having their eyes opened. Keen-seeing business men are recognizing some of the extravagance of the present fictitious standards of the theatre, and as a matter of economy are reducing the system to a more reasonable basis. The star system, which not long ago filled the coffers, has now become a drain. Numberless stars have disappeared from the stage, leaving none to take their places, and several managers are sending out their companies with their own names rather than that of a star outlined in the electric lights. To combat the long run a few experimental repertory theatres have been inaugurated. There has been a movement also to correct some of the old fictitious standards in the placing of the theatres. In many of the cities theatres for legitimate attractions are tending to find place farther from the centre of the city. The artificial standards by which the personality and art of actors are gauged are now repudiated by several of the best of our actors. They have substituted for the personal notice a more dignified form of announcement. A mark of this general though timid tendency toward more veracious standards has been seen in the movement during the past year to reduce the admission fees to some of the better plays.

Another tendency has set in to solve the problem of the one-night stand. We have remarked that when the syndicate system had drawn the life from the provinces, the only theatres that remained vital were the locally managed motion-picture theatres and the vaudeville theatres managed in sectional circuits. The legitimate theatre in the provinces had become moribund where it had not entirely collapsed. But this new tendency which has set in to heal the breach in the legitimate theatre is a tendency to reconstitute the theatre of the provinces on the basis of a narrower social surface. This has come about in the form of local companies and circuits of local companies. During the last three years there has been a tremendous increase in the number of local stock companies. This increase, which is said by some authorities to reach three hundred per cent, is no sporadic thing. It is a healthy movement toward supplying in outlying districts the amusement and art which have been denied under a centralized national system. The significance of this is considerable, for within it there are contained, through its more natural processes of dramatic production, solutions of most of the problems which confront the legitimate theatre to-day.

All these are movements which are taking place within the old institution of the theatre. But there are other tendencies which are moving forward toward a better constitution of things in the drama. These operate by the most rational of all processes, the processes of society itself. They grow out of the fact that the people themselves are taking hold of their dramatic art. In a very real sense the people are taking away from the institution of the theatre functions that have been an institutional monopoly for years. It is as if they said, "The theatre has become alienated from the people. So far has it gone that it misrepresents them, and is socially destructive. In deference to a faculty of human nature itself, we are going to take over to ourselves dramatic activities, and handle them without reference to the old instruments."

And so the people are building a new theatre, fashioned out of their own lives, designed to fit their demands, and to express their standards. Not directly a part of the institution of the theatre, movements are coming up that include, as they should, the old professional theatre in their passion of rebuilding. When these movements are matured, as they will be matured, the theatre itself will stand on a new and broader foundation. How these changes are taking place, the steps that have been taken, the experiments that have been made, and the results that have already been secured would require a larger book than this to tell. Indeed, several books have already appeared to suggest the story. First of all, the people had to learn the theatre. In respect of acquaintanceship with it they were badly handicapped. They had always been shut from the theatre by iron doors. But now they began to study the theatre in the same way that they studied any other social institution that belonged to them, and for which they were responsible. First they began to study the printed play. The publication of plays multiplied at a bound in response to an imperative demand. Closed out of healthy relationship with the theatre as an institution, men and women have been driven to create their theatre for themselves, and they have created it out of books, in circles of readers, in groups gathered together to hear a single reader interpret the play, in any way, indeed, in which they could re-create the healthy and genuine reactions between dramatic art and society.

Undoubtedly all this activity was a temporary thing, and properly so. But men and women were learning dramatic art for themselves, that they might, at the proper time, put their minds to the creating of a better institution of the theatre.

Simultaneously there began the recognition of the dramatic in schools and colleges, the rise of drama clubs for the study of drama, and the organization of drama leagues for the exercise of suasion on the producers of plays. The use of the principles of dramatic art in education has meant more than the discovery on the part of educators that the dramatic method is an efficient method of teaching; it has meant the implicit recognition that drama lies at the very heart of social institutions.

And then came the next and most important step, the formation of independent producing societies of drama all over the country. These producing societies are not at all to be confused with the parlor theatricals of a generation ago. All of them arose from a definite social demand for an immediate expression and participation in dramatic art, and many of them were firmly set to the achieving of better standards and the service of the better social uses of dramatic art. Imperfect as they necessarily were, they derived from their crudeness that wisdom that comes from experiment, and that honesty that rises from the use of original materials. Some of them, as, for instance, the Bohemian Club of California, go back a generation. Many of them are the outgrowths of insistent work during the last few years. In all of them, in so far as they were honest, the necessary things were not a building or even a new repertory, but freedom to experiment, and participation on the part of the audience. That these experimental producing societies, in the Middle West, in Boston, in Philadelphia, have served a purpose is certain. It would not be too much to say that in half a decade they have laid a foundation for a new outlook on American drama. From this movement, as a kind of offshoot, have come the "little theatres" that are springing up in many cities. Not directly connected with the experimental theatre, for by no means all the experimenters of the theatre are wedded to the little-theatre idea, this movement has been an expression of an independent demand aside from the profession of the theatre, that has already risen to a substantial place.

And then apart from these, men and women who would by no means consider themselves experts, or limit their interests to the stage, are turning to the theatre as to a handmaiden. The educator of youth, the teacher of literature and history, the social worker, the playground official are taking drama as an instrument into their work. And even the artist is finding in the drama a means of expression that supplements, or in some respects even replaces, the technique of his own art. Some of the most interesting developments of the recent theatre have come from the adoption of the stage as a studio by those who practice the companion arts.

The rise of the social festival and pageant, the enormous development of the neighborhood spirit in play as well as in work, and the expression of that spirit in terms of the dramatic tradition of the neighborhood, have done much to provide for society those dramatic features so nearly lost through the maleficence of business in the theatre. Society is again discovering its drama in its flower parades, its pageants and festivals, its Fourth of July entertainments, its masques and spectacles. These things have been no sporadic and artificial creation. They have come out of the necessary demands of society for its own expression in play and social art. That they have been outside the theatre has been fortunate both for the theatre and for society. For they have involved a greater degree of participation than the theatre has permitted at any time since its beginnings. They have done much to show that the dramatic faculties are no isolated faculties in individuals, but lie in all men; that this faculty needs to be fostered and developed with the other faculties of the human spirit.

The theatre itself, that great institution that must remain an institution, maintaining its own traditions and respecting its own formulas, will profit greatly from this natural upgrowth. It will gain indirectly in the new quality of participation offered by the audience in the plays presented on the stage. It has already gained much directly in the simpler stories that are told on the stage, in the dash of color and healthy sensationalism that is coming into plays, and in a dependence upon genuine American conditions for its inspiration. One need not go into the changes that may be induced in the form of drama and in theatrical management. This deals too much in prophecy. But there are some things that may safely be promised. The legitimate theatre itself will before long try to adapt itself more closely to those apprehensible social units that lie just behind the institutions of a province. The theatre will cease to try to satisfy an entire national demand and will turn its energies to the service of expression nearer home. Of the vitality of this promise the theatrical experiments in many different parts of the country are excellent witness. In half a dozen neighborhoods efforts of different types are going forward for a new system of provincial organization which shall represent a new type of play production, American, we may hope, to the core, and all the more American because it serves so concretely and expresses so intimately the life of the people of the district from which it springs.

CHAPTER IV

THE THEATRE IN THE OPEN

THE beginnings of things are always outdoors. Likewise when the time for turning has come, and the old must be given up and the new substituted, that change can well take place in the open air. This thought comes to one in thinking of some recent events in the American theatre, and of the place the open-air theatre and the open-air performance are taking in the rejuvenation of our drama. A few years ago we began to hear rumors of what the Bohemian Club of California is doing in its annual open-air performance. And in the University of California a beautiful reproduction of a Greek theatre was built, in which, as time went on, performances of an increasing significance were presented. In some of the colleges the touch of nature was given to dramatic art in the spring festivals and in Shakespearian performances given in the open air at commencement season. Few of us saw the meaning of these events at the time. But gradually they assumed a larger place in the life of the community and took on better value as artistic productions. Later the Ben Greet Players and after them the Coburn Players brought to production in the open air the aid of organization and theatrical experience. We see now that these productons had in them the germ of a new and vital movement which was to do much to renew the soul of the American art of the theatre. To-day the open-air theatre has become a fixed institution of our parks and cities, and before very long society may draw from it something of the native force that inhered in dramatic art in earlier days.

The transfer from the protection of roofs and artificial lights to the free meadow and grove was not taken easily. Strangely enough, we have needed to force ourselves to a sense of the respectability of out-of-doors. It took some time to learn that grown people may play in the open without impropriety, that men may walk the summer streets in shirt waist and without hat, that even a delicate and wise art can prosper in the open air. But we are learning; and it may be that sometime man will again be at home, on his higher as well as his lower sides, amid the surroundings of nature.

There is still a good deal of the "what's the use?" attitude toward dramatics in the open air. We are willing to run, jump, play tennis and golf, walk and ride in the open air during the short months of a Northern summer, but we are apt to ask the question, "Why have an open-air theatre at all since it can be used only four or five months in the year?" It is a strange principle that refuses us the pleasure and use of several delightful months simply because they do not continue throughout the year. Certainly this principle should not be applied to the æsthetic activities if it is not applied to the physical ones. Such a principle rigorously applied would deny us most of the activities of all kinds that make for social health and well-being.

Only the social dreamer dares now venture to state the significance of the open-air theatre in America. This significance is both social and artistic, and in both directions the open-air theatre means an outlet into new and healthier values. To-day this theatre represents much that the established theatre does not do, and much that society needs. On account of its size the open-air theatre is almost necessarily a democratic thing. On account of its character its use represents a spontaneous social demand. By its nature, and the conditions of its building, it belongs to all the people. And its whole disposition is toward the natural and the simple, and the display of the traits of a veritable artistry.

As it now presents itself, the open-air theatre signifies a new movement in dramatic art. On the social side its importance as an outlet for new social promptings, particularly in imaginative directions is highly significant. As it encourages a spontaneous and informal dramatic practice, its character, once it grows to considerable proportions, should be laid permanently in national and provincial characteristics. It would be difficult to import bodily to the stage of an

American open-air theatre an alien motive, and have it keep its flavor of the outlands. There is every reason to hope that the theatre in the open will have no small share in the nationalization of the art of the theatre of America.

The open-air theatre represents to-day one stage in the application of sound social principle to the problem of leisure. This begins in the parks and the playgrounds in the effort to supply sane and healthy opportunities for physical exercise to the children and the men and women of the cities. But good social therapeutics does not cease with physical exercise. As they develop, games tend to become socialized; and as they rise in the scale, they take on more of the characteristics of art. Closely associated with social athletic exercise are the festival and folk ceremonial; and these merge into drama. The ordinary baseball pavilion comes nearer to the form and ideal of the open-air theatre than any other structure in common use in America. If we follow the development of interest in the game of baseball from that of the participant, which we find in the village man, to the objective and dramatic interest of the onlooker, which we see in the city enthusiast, we are led to the conclusion that interest in a dramatic action is but a development of that interest common to all in personal participation in games and exercises. In structure even, the baseball pavilion is more like the theatre of the Greeks than it is like the circus. It is so erected that it faces a centre set in one side rather than the wide area of the stadium.

As a creator of social solidarity the open-air theatre is more effective than any other expedient in use in parks or on campuses. Though the theatre in the open may with propriety appeal only to a few, it achieves its highest function when it is calling together into one mass great numbers of people. The significance of this is great. The forms of amusement in this day are very largely individual. It is only the great national games that draw people together. The automobile, golf, tennis, the pursuit of business and career, all take one away from the social bond. If the open-air theatre can encourage the development of any sense of mass in play it will serve, a significant purpose.

Likewise the open-air theatre should provide a compensating tendency away from the ever-narrowing appeal of the higher types of dramatic art of the city theatres. It provides here in America an expedient for accomplishing what Max Reinhardt is attempting, by somewhat similar means, to accomplish in Germany through the establishment of the "Theatre of the Five Thousand." According to those who see the logic of this step, "Dramatic art will no longer be caviare to the general if it takes the bold step from the theatre to the amphitheatre, from the close confines of the stage to the vast arena of the hippodrome and the circus."

In other ways the open-air theatre will provide an indirect return to society through the type of entertainment that its structure compels. The structure and size of the open-air theatres make necessary simplicity of appeal and a theatric art innocent of casuistries. It adapts itself particularly to certain kinds of performances — the pageant, the chronicle play, the dramatic spectacle; and by the laws of its being the shows and spectacles of the open-air theatre are almost necessarily native and even local.

OPEN-AIR ILLUSION

Perhaps nothing will so clearly indicate the opportunities of the open-air theatre as a statement of the principles under which such a theatre may be used. For this study only a little can now be learned from the methods of production in times when this type of theatre was in common use. Audiences now differ from the audiences of the past, and the modern production, even in the open air, must be adapted to the modern audience. The theories of illusion accepted to-day are so different from those of yesterday that a new modern science of production for open-air theatres has to be worked out. For this science we are in a position to supply now only the elementary principles.

The principle of illusion in the open-air theatre of the present must be based upon its use by a sophisticated city audience. And by a sophisticated audience we mean not only an audience of well-trained minds, but also an audience that has been reared on the conventions of modern stage technique. It does

not seem likely that the use of the open-air theatre
will change greatly the system of illusion and technique now in use on the stage. The theatre will only
discover new mediums and expedients for the practice of that technique, and will by this means enrich
an art that has become formalized, without changing
the principles of that art.

The chief service that this theatre will render
will be to combine the utilization of nature as a medium, or background of dramatic expression, with all
that has been learned of illusion in the theatre through
centuries of experience. If this be accepted as a principle, it will certainly involve some precise specifications in the character of the stage of the open-air
theatre and in the time of the performance.

Under the system of production in the earliest theatres the performances were held in daylight. This
was true in Greece and Rome, and daylight production has been in vogue as late as the time of Elizabeth.
Daylight never offered many opportunities for the
illusion of visual sensation, and when builders began
to enclose their theatres, the time of performance was
pushed later into the day and lighting systems became
of more importance. To-day it may be said that light
stands at the basis of the modern stage illusion. Man-
et's words, spoken for painting, are no less true of the
stage: "The principal personage in modern painting
is the light." Nothing, therefore, would be gained for
society or for the art of the theatre in insisting upon a

system which would run counter to the accustomed systems of illusion. And these to-day demand a performance carved out of darkness, so to speak, by revealing and interpreting rays of light.

Another thing that will be involved in the new theory of the open-air theatre will be the change of the back wall of the stage from the formal lines of the Greek *skene* to a form more adapted to the practice of the modern stage. In consonance with the Greek principles of beauty, the *skene* was adapted to the plastic mode of theatric presentation. With the coming of the stage covering in the late Greek and Roman theatre there began also the movement toward the pictorial type of presentation with scenes and properties. In modern times the same tendency was enhanced by the increased use of artificial lights, which raised the value not only of the action upon the stage, but no less the value of the stage setting, through the playing upon it of illumination. And with the change in lights there went forward also the change in the theories of *rapport* between the audience and the player, involved in the pushing back of the stage behind the proscenium arch, and the consequent achievement of the strict pictorial stage, which since the Restoration in England has been in absolute control of all stage principle. The changed theories of *rapport* of the last few years have been partly influenced by the open-air convention, or at least by the hippodrome order of production. And these years have seen also the development, side by side, of two methods of the theatre, the one the lyrical and recitative method of the earlier open-air theatre and the other the pictorial and conversational method of the enclosed theatre.

There is no expectation that the modern open-air theatre can return to the plastic and lyrical method of the ancient theatre, though already much has been done in that direction. The principle of modern open-air presentation must rest on the convention of night performance under artificial light, the utmost latitude being given for the expressive play of features of nature. The rigid wall of the *skene* must give way to some more flexible background of nature.

The discovery of the dramatic values of the features of nature is distinctly a modern thing. These are now recognized not only as expedients for the securing of primitive effects, but as mediums, which, when handled with understanding and cunning, are capable of some of the richest and most elusive effects in all the domain of art.

Though in every sense an open-air theatre, the theatre of the ancients was built with little eye for the utilization of the effects of nature. It was really of little importance that the audience was seated in the open. In every essential respect the performance might as well have taken place behind closed doors. Not even did the builders of the theatres of Greece pay particular attention to outlook. That they placed

some of their theatres facing the sea seems to have
been an accident. The majority of the theatres were
placed more with reference to convenience in seating than with reference to vista. The late Athenians
erected a high wall behind the Odeum of Herodes
Atticus effectively to shut out the view, and the Ro-
mans in their theatre at Orange denied all chance of
nature background with a high stage wall.

A sophisticated century and a sophisticated people
always discover nature. The discovery, therefore, of
nature as a dramatic medium is naturally a late thing.
It follows man's detachment from nature and his consequent more understanding study and use of her.
The formal gardens of the seventeenth and eighteenth
centuries showed nature taken into man's confidence
again and also made his slave. The Italian theatre
at Villa Gori of the eighteenth century, with its formal
ilex and cypress, disclosed avenues of theatric expressiveness that were closed to the art of the indoor theatre. And no less might the popular playwrights of the
Bankside have learned many lessons of theatric art
from the aristocratic makers of the masques.

For we know now that the open-air theatres of the
present may do for the many what the masques and
the villas of the past did for the few of two centuries
ago. The phenomena of nature and natural objects
are the most adaptable, rich, and suggestive mediums
within reach of man's hand. In versatility, and yet in
fidelity to type, in variety of responsiveness, and

amenability to an exact requirement, no color or line provided by the hand of man can compete with Nature if she is properly schooled. The color value of forest, lake, and field, the shadows thrown by trees and clouds, the light of moon and stars, the varying outline of trees and hills as seen through the changing palpabilities of atmosphere provide infinite material for the stage director. Nature makes no mistakes. Chameleon-like, she adapts herself to the action. Even the falling stars seem to be exquisitely timed. These are matters of optical effect. In auditory effect the open air is no less rich. It would be impossible for a bird to sing in the wrong place in "As You Like It." The interspersed silences and insect voices of the night are both fitly chosen for their parts.

The director of a play in the open air has the delightful sense of working with powers beyond himself that will bring forth beauties better than his thought. The surprises and the discoveries of the art are a part of its rich compensation. For the open air remains one of the unspoiled mediums of dramatic art.

TYPES OF OPEN AIR THEATRES

Enough has been said to suggest roughly the principles of structure and use favored by the writer. For several reasons these principles tend away from the rigorous historical orders and toward the substitution for them of something new and more adapted to present conditions. A study of certain present types of

open-air theatre may serve to support these conclusions. Experiments have been made in the structure
and use of two or three characteristic forms of such
theatres in this country, and from these we will draw
our theories.

Logically the earliest type of theatre in the open
would be a natural amphitheatre unchanged by man.
Ordinarily the ground would present two grades either
a slope from which the audience would look down over
the stage, or a stage set on a hillside backed by the
rise of the hill up to which the audience would look.
Though logically the earliest form, in practice this
type of theatre requires a very high type of theatric
imagination for its successful use, and much more
skilled and scientific stage management than is permitted on the austere stage of the Greeks. It may be
taken as a principle that the more we depend upon
nature the more skilled and sophisticated the stage
management must be.

By all means the best type of this theatre in use in
America is the Grove of the Bohemian Club in California which has now been in use for thirty-eight years.
A consideration of the work of the Bohemian Club
requires a treatise in itself. Those interested are
referred to a book by Porter Garnett, privately printed
by the Bohemian Club, entitled "The Bohemian
Jinks," and the introduction to "The Green Knight"
by the same writer. From the former the following
extracts are quoted: —

It is nine o'clock at night when the performance begins. Six hundred men are gathered in a spacious glade of the redwood forest. Rows of redwood logs are used for seats. All is darkness save for a group of tiny shaded lights that make the figures of the men and their surroundings dimly visible. They are the lights for the musicians in the orchestra pit. Behind them is a stage innocent of scenery except that provided by Nature. On either side of this stage two immense trees forming the proscenium stretch upward into the greater darkness overhead. At the back of the stage is an abrupt hillside covered with a dense growth of shrubs and small trees, picked out here and there with the shafts of redwood. Amid the tangle of brake and brush, the trail which the eye can scarcely see by day winds its devious course.

Slowly, mysteriously, the only curtain — which is one of darkness — is lifted, and the stage is lighted by artificial means, cunningly disguised, augmenting the placid rays of the moon. The action of the play begins.

The stage is situated at the foot of a wooded hillside, and, as has been already said, is framed by the trunks of enormous trees that form a natural proscenium. In front is an orchestra pit large enough to accommodate the fifty or more musicians employed in the production. . . . The hillside rises abruptly from the back of the stage, and on it is a series of platforms, completely masked by foliage, where parts of the action take place. The stage, or set of stages, which calls for and admits of, different treatment from all others, has its chiefest dissimilarity in what may be called its vertical character. The action may take place here, not at one, two, or three elevations, but at ten or even more if necessary. It is possible of course to compass on such a stage effects that cannot be produced in the ordinary theatre, and the productions invented for it are usually shaped to its magnificent possibilities.

The hillside is a natural sounding board and the acoustics of the place are so good that words spoken in a normal tone from the highest point of the trail by a person whose voice has ordinary carrying power, can be distinctly heard at the back of the auditorium glade.

From this study of the California Grove amphitheatre we get the following points: —

1. Performances are held at night and are accompanied by an unusual degree of mechanical and illuminative artifice.

2. As many as possible of the effects are gained from the manipulation and use of natural objects.

3. The very individuality of the stage serves as a limitation on the kinds of plays that can be successfully produced. These must be written expressly for the club, and must be adapted to the wild type of its stage. Here it is not the austerity of man's edifice, but the overpowering character of nature itself that limits the producer.

Next to this is the so-called "Greek" theatre type with a stage background of hard classic lines, adapted to the Greek ideals of art and standing for the plastic type of production. To this is related the Roman theatre in which the audience is brought nearer to the stage, the stage is elevated, the incline of seats is raised, and all the indications point to the development of the more recent principles of dramatic production. The most famous American example of a theatre combining characteristics of both these types is the well-known Hearst Greek Theatre of the University of California.

The Hearst Greek Theatre is an excellent example of modern fidelity to ancient type. The impression the building gives is one of chaste dignity and beauty. The building itself is so impressive that some of the excellent advantages of its location against a tree-covered hillside are lost. The stage is wide and shallow, being twenty-eight feet deep, one hundred and thirty-three feet in long dimension, and five feet high. The containing walls of concrete, ornamented with Doric pilasters, and pierced by five doors, run up to the height of forty-two feet. The seats of the amphitheatre rise in concentric circles to the same height.

The building is, therefore, a massive concrete and masonry bowl of remarkably pure and strong beauty. Its one great shortcoming is the fact that it forces on the producer a servility to the classic type of production. Let me quote from a careful study of the principles of this building made by Mr. Kenneth Sawyer Goodman: —

I at once found myself wondering just what use an American playwright or pageanteer could make of such a theatre without constantly feeling the limitations put upon him by all this background of solid masonry. Clearly the eye could not be tricked into accepting any illusion of distance, of depth of picture, attempted no matter how simply, or cleverly. Clearly the sides of the frame could in no way be narrowed without screening the greater part of the remaining stage area from the view of at least half the audience. No change of setting could be accomplished on a stage which could not be well curtained, and which owing to the color of the material would never be completely dark save on the blackest of moonless nights. It was obvious too, that no large piece of scenery could be handled through the narrow doors already mentioned, and that the problem of lighting would always be complex and difficult.

I decided reluctantly, for I admired the beauty of the place, that it could be used effectively only for the presentation of dramatic forms closely allied to the Greek play in structure, or at best hampered by some equally rigid convention. As I look at the range of plays, masques, and pageants already written or still to be written which are, or will be played in the open air I cannot be too emphatic in stating my objection to such limitations and conventions. It should be possible, first of all, to stage chronicle plays dealing with American history, European history, the history of art, letters, etc. This cannot be done without suggesting glimpses of forests, streets, squares, gardens, house-fronts, even now and then a Hall of Justice, or the throne room of a palace. We must therefore be able to change our background, either to darken or to curtain our stage for that purpose and to deepen or narrow the acting area as occasion demands. None of these things can be accomplished successfully at Berkeley.

A study of the plays produced in the Greek Theatre strengthens our agreement with Mr. Goodman's conclusions. Those plays which have been produced with absolute success have been the tragedies of the immortal trio of Greece. Where modern romantic plays were produced the stage was not used at all, but the action was brought down into the orchestra, and the stone columnar background was hidden as well as might be with trees.

The chief drawbacks of the Greek Theatre at Berkeley for the purposes of an American open-air theatre are: —

1. Its inflexible requirement of a certain alien type of production.

2. Its lack of facilities for effective night illumination.

3. Its failure to appropriate the natural characteristics of the district to its own purposes, and its consequent neglect of any national or provincial character.

A Greek theatre which avoids some of these limitations is the theatre of the Theosophical Society at Point Loma, California, the first theatre of the type in America. This theatre utilizes the natural characteristics of location by providing a magnificent marine outlook. The presence of a small Greek temple is the only thing that controls the type of production.

From these two illustrations we may without further discussion derive certain principles of open-air theatre construction.

The open-air theatre should be the product of the environment, both as to society, and as to natural surroundings.

The stage should be so manipulated that it will be subordinate to, and not superior to, the interests of the action.

Such a theatre should show the following characteristics: —

1. A maximum of the sense of open air as compared with the comparative structural enclosure of the classical type.

2. A background sufficiently flexible and enigmatical to serve the diverse purposes of illusion.

3. A background sufficiently appropriate to express the national and provincial character of the environment.

The last two requirements sufficiently clearly point to a background of trees or an appropriate vista of lake or sea or mountain. The cypresses and ilex of the Villa Gori in Italy; the willows of Professor Behren's theatre at Dusseldorf, Germany; the pine woods of the natural stage of the pageant at Peterborough, the redwoods and eucalyptus of California, the hickories, walnuts, and elms of the Middle West, are all thoroughly appropriate, from the point of view of illusion no less than of local color.

BUILDING TECHNIQUE

It is already clear that the building technique of an open-air theatre will depend largely on the physical characteristics of the ground under consideration. If in a hilly country, the theatre should be placed on the side of a hill. If in a flat country, the amphitheatre may be scooped out saucer-shaped from a meadow. The stage should always be set with due relation to background, and this should always be natural. No building should be permitted within the vista. Where there is water it is well that the stage should be contiguous to the water, so that boats, gondolas, even water nymphs may be used in the action. Of the latter qualification the open-air theatre erected in Forest Park, St. Louis, for the Historic Masque and Pageant of St. Louis in the summer of 1914, provides an excellent illustration. Here the vast stage was built on poles over an inland lake with a broad ribbon of clear water before the stage which served not only for marine action but as a sounding-board. In short, the topography of the ground, and the presence of natural features, should govern in every case, and the rule should be: Nature manipulated only to discover its best values, and make it tractable.

In theory the open-air theatre should be large, but its size is not a binding characteristic. Indeed, if the construction of the theatre is not too formal, its size is easily flexible. Unlike an indoor auditorium, the open-air theatre is amenable to treatment in units, and it is the audience that supplies the standard of completeness rather than the building. A small audience well grouped around the stage is as complete in itself as a larger one. Ordinarily no open-air theatre should be built in park or campus that will not permit large crowds. The open-air theatres in estates and private parks are a different thing.

It is usually found that one's estimate of areas is

less trustworthy outdoors than indoors. So one is likely to underestimate rather than overestimate the seating capacity of a given plot of ground. Given a square of two hundred and fifty feet there is easily room for a stage and amphitheatre seating ten thousand spectators. The size of the open-air theatre is really limited only by the acoustic properties of the plat, and the illusionistic theories accepted.

The matter of acoustics is very much more simple outdoors than indoors. Outdoors it is simply a matter of experiment until a good place is found. Indoors the factors are far more complicated, and at the best are subject to ungovernable chance. As a rule the voice carries better in the open air, and this is particularly the case where the amphitheatre is a natural one. The Greek Theatre at Berkeley is situated in a natural depression in the University campus known as "Weede's Hollow," because of the discovery by a student named Weede of the wonderful acoustic properties of the place.

The seats in the amphitheatre may be arranged in either straight or concentric lines. The latter is the plan of the Greek theatres, and is followed by almost all open-air theatres. There are spots in which the demands of the situation seem to require straight lines. The floor surface of the amphitheatre should be inclined in any case (unless as in the case of the Bohemian Club stage, which itself is on a hillside, and faces a very small open amphitheatre.) In a flat country undue excavating and building may be avoided by making the surface saucer-shaped. In the Greek Theatre at Berkeley there are two lines of incline, the more radical being at a distance, the gentler sloping toward the stage. In arranging the surface of the auditorium care needs to be taken of the lines of sight. These are compounded of the factors of the height of the stage, the incline of the amphitheatre with heights of seats, and the distance between the rows of seats.

STAGE

We have before decided against the rigid lines of the Greek *skene* as unadaptable to American uses, and have also shown that the plays must be given at night with a certain acknowledgment of the claims of the modern convention. This brings us to several questions: First, What will take the place of the frame provided by the side walls of the Greek *skene*, and by the proscenium arch of the closed theatre? Second, Since the plays are to be performed at night, by what means will sufficient light be provided to illuminate the scene?

As it happens, the answer to these questions is a single one. The proscenium arch is no accidental and arbitrary thing. It has entered into the theory not only of the theatre, but of the action of the play. If the open-air theatre is to be true to modern convention it must provide a frame for the picture. It may be a tree on each side of the stage, or a pole or a wicker arch. Such a frame is, for instance, provided beautifully by the trees of the Bohemian Grove stage. The answer to the double question is contained in the suggestion to erect at the right and the left of the stage and at its front line two high lighting towers, of characteristic architecture, provided with platforms at the top from which the lighting board can be handled. By this means and by the use of hidden footlights, borders swung on wires behind branches, and calciums properly distributed, all the lighting effects that are required on any stage may be secured. At the same time the towers will serve as effective frames for the action.

The size of the stage is not a fixed quantity. We saw that the Berkeley stage measures twenty-eight by one hundred and thirty-three feet. These dimensions hardly stand the test of experience. Ordinarily fifty by seventy-five feet is the proper size, but this should be subject to easy increase by annexing portions of the amphitheatre in front. In fact, this has had to be done in the performances in the Berkeley Greek Theatre. Given a stage of forty feet depth and an available fore-stage extension of fifty feet and one has an available stage depth of ninety feet, certainly more than enough for a usual use. The length of the stage may vary greatly. In case of the use of large numbers of people they can be used in processional. And any greater length than seventy feet provides problems of sight from all parts of the enclosure that are hardly worth the advantage gained. It must be confessed that these figures are dwarfed by the size of the great St. Louis stage, which was five hundred feet broad and faced an amphitheatre seating eighty thousand people. At most there would hardly be demand for more than two or three such theatres in the country.

As to background of the stage we have perhaps said enough to show that in the present state of the open-air theatre in America no high wall or building could be considered appropriate. There is nothing better than a background of trees sufficiently dense to appear solid, and sufficiently open to give vistas beyond of hills or lake. Each location has its own problems which should be made its opportunities. If the stage is on a level with the ground it will not even need a balustrade, but if it is above ground a simple protection will be required, broken by entrances from off the stage. Of all entrances the side entrances should be most ample, as they must give opportunity for the simultaneous entrance of many people, of chariots and animals. Steps should not be used as entrances if it is possible to avoid them.

Soon we may expect that the planting of trees as background and as side enclosures will be undertaken in a formalistic way. There are some American trees, such as the evergreens and the poplars, which are subject to formal uses, and these may be planted and trimmed to suit the style of the theatre. The use, too, of hedges and bushes for side protecting walls is to be recommended. The principle is wherever possible to use the expedients of nature under the manipulative treatment of man.

The stage proper is constructed of masonry or concrete. The stage floor may be covered with oiled macadam or be sodded, according to the floor of the amphitheatre. In dispensing with the Greek *skene* we lose the ancient place for the dressing-rooms. These may be placed in clumps of trees to right and left, away from the line of sight, or, where the stage is on a hill, they may be placed under the stage. Nothing is gained by having the dressing-rooms immediately contiguous to the stage. Indeed, under the informal convention of the open air there is an added charm in having the dressing-rooms at such a distance that the players may be observed walking to their places.

Very little can be said about the cost of an open-air theatre. This detail depends upon the local situation and demand. The work may involve only the grading and seeding of a grass meadow and turf stage, or it may rise to the ambitious heights of granite construction. A community which seriously desires an open-air theatre can get one which serves all purposes for two thousand dollars aside from cost of land.

USES OF OPEN-AIR THEATRES

The agitation for open-air theatres has accompanied a development in certain types of dramatic art. As a rule these types have arisen apart from the commercial theatre and in response to a spontaneous demand on the part of the people. When the open-air theatre comes to pass, it will find ready for it whole orders of dramatic practice which need but its facilities to bring them to perfection.

The pageant which has been reborn in England and America within the last ten years is now one of the most influential types of dramatic art. The pageants of Sherborne, Oxford, York, and Warwick in England, the pageants of Norwich, of Bronxville, of Cornish, New Rochelle, Quebec, Gloucester, Rochester, Detroit, Peterborough, the Northwest, and St. Louis, have led the way for pageants in the great cities and in scattered hamlets. Beginning almost spontaneously in scattered places as processions and ceremonials, they soon took the necessary step into dramatic form. Produced at first upon rude or improvised stages, the time has come when they demand the facilities which will give them a proper staging.

But even better than the pageant for the uses of the open-air theatre is the masque. This is a form which, more dependent on machinery and mass effects than the pageant, and less controlled by the idea and the necessities of naturalism, offers opportunities of the widest appeal through all the instrumentalities of music, dancing, scenery, color, lighting, and plastic effects. The pageant is still bound to the individual as actor, and the individual is likely to be dwarfed on the open-air stage. But the masque operates through massed groups, through symbolic scenery, through ballets and processions, and through the now hardly realized possibilities of the *Uebermarionette*.

The open-air theatre is not made for fine psychological effects delivered to the intelligence. But it is an open door to the soul of the senses. Anything that appeals to the sensibilities, whether in the finer spiritual or in the more sensuous zones, finds a place there. For this reason the fanciful, the symbolic, the fantastic, the pantomimic, even horse-play and pretty romping, are at home on its stage. Harlequin and Columbine, Punchinello and Pickle Herring, Pastor Fido and Aminta, Jaques and Audrey, and Bottom and Theseus, and their modern counterparts belong to the open-air theatre.

We in America have made a start toward this kind of writing. The pastoral plays and the fantastics and masques of Percy MacKaye, "the Jinks" of the Bohemian Club, the masques of Stevens and Goodman, and very many others of local import show the way in which the movement is headed.

Every day the newspapers bring us suggestions of new open-air meeting-places for the people. Many of these are only suggestions, but some of them will be achieved. The open-air theatre will be but another instrument for the reconstruction of American dramatic art by a saner social plan.

CHAPTER V

FESTIVALS AND PAGEANTRY

AMONG the social developments of the past ten years none has been more significant than the rapid growth of pageantry. Ten years ago the pageant was known only as an obsolete ceremonial, continued in the vestiges of the street parade, the carnival, and the secret-society ritual. To-day the largest cities and the smallest villages have their pageants. The pageant has woven its way into the fabric of society. It is now a commonplace that the pageant is a potent instrument in the social programme. And by its zealous adherents it is hailed as an early expression of an art impulse springing from the soil.

The significance of the pageant is thus a dual one. On the one side it signifies an active society seeking an outlet for its common energies. On the other side it represents an appropriation on a large scale by the people themselves of new agencies of artistic expression, aside from those provided by the theatre, and their use of these agencies for their own purposes and according to their own methods.

Along with the pageant there have also grown up other ceremonies which, like the pageant, are also in the people's hands, and are being used for social and artistic purposes. These are the festival, on the art side standing lower than the pageant, and the masque, which ranks æsthetically higher. All of these function in the same way. All of them are outdoor activities, they all require the participation of many people in exercises directed toward social unity in the forms of art expression, and all of them involve new systems of organization for the purposes of this expression.

To one who is able to read the signs of the times this rise of pageantry and the outdoor ceremonial spells important meanings, not only for the present, but for the future of American society and American dramatic art. For here we have a spontaneous and a native movement which is part and parcel of the American system. The principles of pageantry have not been laid down by external regulation. They have developed normally out of the active practice of the art. A study of the principles underlying pageantry will do much to make clear the tendencies now forming for a more coherent society and its expression by a native art.

THE SUBSTANCE OF PAGEANTRY

Manifestly such a study cannot begin with a definition. This must be supplied by a consideration of the art itself in its historical development and in its various kinds. There would probably be agreement among those who practice the art of pageantry as to the general substance of which the pageant is constructed.

The following are suggested as the material of pageantry: —

1. *Historical fact.* It may be agreed that every pageant is composed of social material which may be identified by reference to history. This material usually centres around certain definite events or outstanding or significant persons. The great majority of pageants of all kinds contain such substance.

2. *Ceremonial and form.* These differ from historical fact in that they are the ordered expressions of past social practices, the ornate dress of social activities, the symbols of dignities and classes. This material is full of light for the historian. It is indispensable to the artist and lover of humanity. There is a tendency on the part of some to belittle this element in the pageant. This is an essential mistake. A true pageant requires ceremonial and form. Some ages are ceremonial of themselves. For them pageantry is a part of existence. Other ages have little ceremonial. These call upon the pageant master to imitate past forms, and to invent new ones.

3. *Folk-activities and folk-lore.* These are the outgrowth of the primitive imaginations of men. But primitive imagination belongs no more to early than to late times. The primitive imagination is always at work. It is the task of the pageant master to perpetuate the past and to formulate for art the more recent. The stories and dances of all times, the heroic and

COURTLY AND DRAMATIC PAGEANTRY

Though we have discovered the substance of the pageant and what it is not, we have not yet discovered what a pageant is. For we find that historically there are several types of ceremonies of widely different origin to which the term "pageant" can properly be applied. These must be studied for the light they will throw on the later developments of pageantry.

First in order is what may be called "courtly pageantry." This type quite appropriately comes first, not only because it is the earliest in time, but because its principle is found as an influence in all types of pageantry even down to the present. Courtly pageantry differed from many forms of modern pageantry in that it was a solemn function and expression of constituted authority. As a feature of court life pageantry was no mere pastime or festival exercise. It was the outward symbol of the glories of the court, or the mystery and power of the Church.

In courtly pageantry there were always two parties; those who in their own persons represented the dignity honored; and that larger number who as spectators and as marching legions did homage in providing color and numbers. Pageantry was thus no unimportant instrument in keeping alive the illusion of royalty. It was not for nothing that the Master of the Revels was a high functionary in the court. He was, indeed, a prop and support of the crown. And in addition to fostering the divine right of kings the courtly pageant provided much of the social and artistic stimulation of the time. The universal appetite for stirring ceremonies was satisfied as a feature of the common organization of society.

In form the courtly pageant was usually a procession executed either in the street, or in a church, or in a room at court. The pageant was given on the occasion of a visit of the sovereign to a town. The ceremony itself was called a "riding." The earliest recorded pageant of this type is that given in 1236 to King Henry III and Eleanor of Provence on the occasion of their trip from London to Westminster. In 1377, King Richard II was received by the citizens of London with a pageant which has been described by Walsingham. An early author of a pageant was Lydgate, who wrote in honor of King Henry IV a part of the Pageant of Agincourt. A riding "against" Queen Margaret, wife of Henry VI, occurred at Coventry in 1455 in which there was representation of nine worthies including King Arthur. Margaret, Queen of Scotland, was welcomed to Aberdeen by a pageant in which the great Emperor Bruce offered addresses. At the coronation of Queen Elizabeth there was a pageant representing the joining of the houses of Lancaster and York. And the subsequent progresses of Elizabeth and James are famous.

As has been said, these pageants were usually arrested processions in which gratulatory addresses were exchanged and some verses recited. Among the early dramatists of the courtly pageants were Peele, Munday, and Dekker. Many of the chief pageants of the Elizabethan age and of the seventeenth century were water pageants. Scott has described in "Kenilworth" the water pageantry of Elizabeth. Evelyn tells us of a magnificent water pageant which was given to greet the consort of Charles II, Catherine of Braganza, as she came to London from Hampton Court, August 23, 1662. They came in an "antique-shaped open boat, covered with a state or canopy of cloth of gold, made in form of a cupola, supported with high Corinthian pillars wreathed with flowers, festoons, and garlands."

Among the chief water pageants were the Lord Mayor's Pageants which began in 1454, and were given on Lord Mayor's Day every year for almost four hundred years. These pageants were first described in 1533. For this pageant magnificent barges were supplied by the city trading companies, by the municipality, and by the court. The title of Queen's Waterman was retained in the reign of Queen Victoria long after the last Lord Mayor's Pageant had been given in the early forties. The Lord Mayor's Pageant has been very recently revived.

Few of the more lavish ceremonies of court life were revived after the Civil War. Even the coronation has to-day little of its former grandeur. The expense of coronations fell from two hundred and forty thousand pounds for George IV to less than one quarter of that

sum for Victoria and Edward. To-day the greatest
official pageant is found in the reviewing of troops
on land and of the fleet on sea. The courtly pageant
had an influence in setting the standard of pageantry
in other unofficial quarters. But as it has passed away,
its place has had to be taken by other forms of pageantry which are more adapted to the social principles
of present days.

At this point we find the history of the pageant involved in the history of modern drama. To trace the
early history of either the pageant or the drama would
lead one very far into the ill-defined activities of primitive people. Probably both pageantry and drama as
social activities arose from the same impulse that gave
the courtly ceremonial such a strong hold over the
imaginations of men. It would seem that both pageantry and drama arose from the liturgy of the Church,
an institution that, like the court, maintained its dignity by means of ceremony, but, unlike the court, was
more socially constituted, and therefore gave greater
openings for social initiative.

The means whereby the pageant developed from the
church liturgy through the miracle plays on Biblical
subjects to later secular drama belong as much to the
field of history of drama as of pageantry. The very
early Corpus Christi plays, the later York and Town-
ley mysteries, the Coventry plays done by the trading
companies of the shearmen and tailors were called
pageants. These pageants had many of the features

lately associated with pageantry. They were the real-istic representation of records, more or less authentic; they were produced by the community; and they were in the form of processions on wagons, the action usu-ally taking place at central points where the wagons were brought to rest.

But these pageants still lacked an indispensable element, that of the native historical record. This be-gins to appear even in the religious drama when the Biblical story is changed for a native story. As early as 1416 there is record of a pageant of St. George acted before Emperor Sigismund and Henry V on the occasion of the visit of the former to Westminster. This production was in three parts: First, the arming of St. George; second, St. George riding and fighting with the Dragon; third, St. George and the King's daughter leading the lamb in at the castle gates. With Robin Hood pageants we come still nearer to native elements. These were based on ballads, and date back to 1475 and 1550. With the Hock Tuesday Play of Coventry the martial element appears in the glorify-ing of the life and death of a historic hero. It is not known whether this play commemorates the death of Hardicanute in 1042 or the massacre of St. Brice in 1102. It was certainly performed as early as 1416, and was seen by Elizabeth at Kenilworth in 1575. Little is known of its production save Laneham's witness that it was expressed in "actions and rhymes." By this time the art of the pageant, like that of drama, was becoming complex, composed in part of debased imitations of courtly ceremonies and in part of genuine folk-lore elements. In the Midsummer Eve Plays, and the Hock Tuesday Plays, later in the interludes and chronicles, there were mingled, with episodes as pathetic as Bottom's ill-fated venture in dramatic production, intrinsic elements of real social worth.

It is now but a step to the chronicle play. With this there is added the last substance necessary to the pageant. For our purposes the chronicle play begins with "The Tragedy of the King of Scots," 1567, "to the which belonged the scenery of Scotland and the great castle on the other side." After this play, which has been lost, come "The Famous Victories of Henry V," "The Life and Death of Jack Straw," "The Troublesome Reign of King John of England," and chronicle plays by Peele, Marlowe, Shakespeare, and other dramatists. Though no claim is made that these were pageants, they were like pageants in many respects. They were based on actual chronicles, closely adhered to; they were loosely constructed in series of scenes; they were concerned with the externals of history, its battles, marchings, and triumphal crises. Though they belonged to the theatre, they reflected the more social temper of pageantry.

RECENT HISTORY OF PAGEANTRY

It will not take long to deal with the later history of pageantry. The court of James I was highly ceremonial, and pageantry flourished in court and on the stage of the theatre. With the great Civil War, pageantry practically disappeared, and the dull level of the theatre of the eighteenth century reflects the collapse of the older festivals and ceremonies and the lack of the sensational and colorful in social life. The beginnings of pageantry of the nineteenth century are derived from the increased interest in chivalry and the antique, of which romanticism was the expression and the impulse. The man who, above all, was responsible was Sir Walter Scott, who in his novels presented a panorama of the past, and in "Ivanhoe," "The Talisman," and "Kenilworth" describes in detail old pageant ceremonies.

One pageant of the nineteenth century was of great note for reasons that will appear. Undoubtedly the romances of Scott were the general inspiration of the Eglinton Tournament, but the proximate impulse must have come from the coronation of Queen Victoria two years before. The dashing young Earl of Eglinton had been present at the coronation and soon thereafter called rehearsals for a magnificent tournament at the Eyre Arms Hotel, west of London. When the tournament was given late in August, 1834, all of the actors and spectators were transported to Eglinton Castle near Irvine in Scotland. The pageant was made up of chivalric ceremonials, tourneys of horsemanship, processions of gayly costumed nobles and ladies led by a marshall, and the crowning of the Queen of Beauty amid her maids of honor. The total expenditure was said to reach forty thousand pounds. Among those who took part was the young Prince Louis Napoleon, later to be Emperor of the French, who engaged in a tilting match with Mr. Charles Lamb. The Queen of Beauty was the granddaughter of Sheridan, the beautiful Lady Seymour, later the Duchess of Somerset.

Even the weather was cruel to this first modern pageant. It was given for three days under pouring rain with spirits that drooped like the damp feathers. What spirit was left was soon dissipated by the ridicule evoked. The prints and lampoons of the romantic age of English literature were far more censorious of this type of entertainment than are the critics of our later age of reason. A burlesque tournament was held in Oxfordshire. Thackeray found occasion to ridicule Louis Napoleon: "like Mr. Pell's friend in 'Pickwick' in a suit of armor and silk stockings." Disraeli made it the crowning piece of descriptive satire of his novel "Endymion," as Scott has made his description of Leicester's revels for Elizabeth the crowning piece of romance of "Kenilworth." Not for seventy-five years did British aristocracy attempt another tournament.

The last gasp of the aristocratic pageant was in the Southern States of America. Among those who attended the Eglinton Pageant was William Gilmer, of Maryland. Returning to his home he prepared in 1840 a chivalric tournament at The Vineyard, his country place outside of Baltimore. A similar tournament was given at Cowpens, the villa of the Howards, a little later, and still another in 1850. One of the last was given at Front Royal in Virginia in 1866. Tournaments with pageant elements have not been uncommon in the reconstructed South, but here again Civil War was a fatal intervention. For later exercise we must go to the folk-festivals, the celebration of Guy Fawkes Day in New England, the carnivals of New Orleans, and the flower *festas* of California, none of which are pageants in the true sense.

The precise forces that brought about the abrupt birth of the modern democratic pageant in 1905 are not apparent. It is clear enough that the general forces were the social and artistic reawakening which came with the beginning of the century. The man who deserves credit for giving the first twentieth-century pageant is the dramatist Louis Napoleon Parker, who in 1905 prepared a pageant for Sherborne, Dorset, England, in commemoration of the twelve hundredth anniversary of the founding of the city. Other pageants soon followed at Warwick, York, and Oxford. The same month and year in which the Sherborne Pageant was given, June, 1905, Percy MacKaye and others gave the Saint-Gaudens Pageant in Cornish. Strictly, this was probably more masque than pageant. The Educational Pageant of the State Normal School in Boston, the Philadelphia Pageant or procession in honor of the two hundred and twenty-fifth anniversary of the founding of the city, and the Quebec Pageant were all held in 1908. Of these only the Quebec Pageant possessed both historical and dramatic elements. The Pageant of the Italian Renaissance, given in Chicago in January, 1909, lacks the native element, but should be accorded place as the first chronicle pageant produced in the United States.

Of the general mass of present-day pageants there remain two classes which are of widely different character. The first of these is the so-called "Continental" or "Processional" type of pageant, in which the event and the ceremony are represented in a moving procession of floats and symbolic figures in costume.

The second is the English or dramatic type, in which the action takes place on one spot, or on a series of related spots, in the form of a plot loosely constructed of a series of authentic episodes in dramatic form, usually comprising speech, action, and suggestive setting.

Both of these types of pageant have their defenders. The chief recent defender of the processional type of pageant is Dr. Ellis Paxson Oberholtzer, who gave the Philadelphia Pageant in 1908. In behalf of this is cited the historical fact that all pageants began in the processional, first of church ceremony, later of wagons and traveling stages. There is also mentioned the fact that this type can reach a far greater number of people than can the dramatic pageant.

In spite of some advantages for the procession, the trend of argument and critical favor seems to be toward the dramatic type. While the advocates of the dramatic pageant grant that historically the procession came first, they assert that in every case in which the ceremony was permitted to develop the pageant became dramatic. In other words, the procession first became an arrested procession, and gradually the value of the rests came to overshadow the value of the moving parade. In the early pageant plays of the guilds of England the wagon, which first had been a float, becomes next a stage, and finally, after fixed stages had been introduced, became a servile carrying vehicle. The same tendency is seen in the French pageant. The Pageant of Orléans began as a procession and before it had gone far had become a stage show.

THE SOCIAL PRINCIPLES OF PAGEANTRY

Our study of the substance and history of the pageant has brought to light certain principles which must be observed if the pageant is to reach the highest effectiveness. At the outset it is granted that the pageant is not one of the more rigorously formal types of art. Indeed, its informality, and its general adaptability, are its great advantages as an instrument of social art. But this informality of pageant structure should not be carried too far. The pageant needs to be particularly guarded against slipshod workmanship, for by nature it has little inherent structure to hold it together.

One principle that has already been discovered is

that it is important to distinguish the pageant from other festival-art forms. This must be done as well for the purposes of effectiveness of the pageant as for its social usefulness. Often committees announce pageants when they mean merely ornamented picnics, and they wonder why the plans of the director fail to harmonize with their own. To them he may seem unbending and rather presumptuous in his demands that all plans converge in his. But the pageant must be the centre of the festival. It may well be a feature of a fête-day, but it must be the culminating feature. And above all the fête must not be called a pageant. Loose as it may be in its lines the pageant is not a form of activity that will coöperate in a three-ring circus arrangement.

And so it is important that the pageant shall be used only when the pageant is called for, and that when used the pageant shall be given right of way. And upon what festival occasion is a pageant called for? It is demanded only when it is required that some communication shall be made to the audience through the medium of the festival. Like all other arts the pageant is an art of focus. It should be given only when it is desired to draw together into one representation the spirit of a day or an occasion. For this reason it is particularly appropriate to give pageants in commemoration of historical events. It is one of the chief advantages of the pageant as a social ceremonial that it joins a true play spirit with this ability to focus lines of thought. But the pageant is not satisfied with play, and when used for this purpose alone always fails. It is for the committee to decide whether the occasion calls for games or pageantry.

Another principle that must be observed in pageantry is that the social is more important than the individual. Though it belongs in the class of dramatic art, the pageant differs from drama in that, while drama deals with the fortunes of individuals and through them of the mass, the pageant is primarily concerned with the mass and secondarily with the individual. The virtue of the pageant is that it can portray the surfaces of great movements and the relations of parties. In this respect the pageant is the dramatic correspondent of the epic. And like the epic its structure is one of spirits and magnitudes rather than of individuals.

The looseness of the structure of the pageant is the result of this, and it is an aid in the expression of these generalized groups. The action is altogether an external one and is composed, not of struggles of organized forces, but of a series of social phenomena. When there is struggle, it is the clash of large material groups, battles of armies, attacks of forts, the scaling of walls. In this there is no room for the play of motive or of individual impression. The individual man is merged in his race.

In the same sense that the social is more important than the individual, the ceremony is more important than the event. The pageant works through the instrument of the most palpable effect. Just as the comedy of manners is built on the theory that through the convention of manners the inner truths of man are revealed, the pageant is raised on the principle that through his ceremonies we come to know man himself. Between the important event detached from any of the formalities of ceremony and the less important event which is clothed in the vestments of convention, the skilled pageant master always chooses the latter, knowing that it will speak more clearly to a large number. When you take the ceremonial out of the pageant you take the thing that most justifies it and makes it impressive.

Though the pageant refers away from the individual to society, and from the event to the ceremony, it must not be inferred that it refers away from the concrete. The pageant is above all the art of concrete representation in its larger magnitudes. It should not at all be confused with those forms of dramatic art which represent the idea by an abstract symbol. The purpose of the pageant is the re-creation of authentic mass effects, not the illumination of a general theme by the machinery of suggestion. In other words, the entire structure of the pageant should be historically on the ground. As T. W. Stevens has said, "The pageant itself will be, of necessity, a sympathetic treatment of history, a visualization of the past, set forth moment by moment, in appearance true to the record and fact. It should be as easy to follow as a well-devised chronicle play. In its way it has a certain literalness. It puts the observer in possession of the sequence of characters and forces which have made history."

But here, lest one may be misled by the precept of concreteness, as many are, and suppose that a pageant may be made of any series of historical events however selected, another word of warning must be spoken. All scenes of a pageant should have some impelling force within. This impelling force may come from the clash of contending forces; it may come from the sympathy aroused in the audience by the associations of a famous historical episode, either of heroism, of sacrifice, or of portent; it may come from scenes which involve a great deal of ceremony and color and grace in display; or it may be evoked by the appropriate use of stirring music.

This requirement shuts out many scenes of purely *verbatim* historical discussion. An episode may be historically never so important, and if it lacks dramatic force it cannot be used in pageantry. "Mere talk" is seldom effective in the pageant. Where words are used they must be the orations, the pronunciamentos, the quick give-and-take of challenge. This eliminates also the contemporary scenes of everyday life. In fact there is little if any room for the present day in the theme of pageantry. For natural scenes are invariably on a lower order of emotional appeal than the scenes of the past. There is for them no social uniformity of attitude. It is also quite impossible to act these by the code of acting in use in pageantry. It seems safe to say that no event that comes within the lives of the generation now living is appropriate for pageant treatment. It is only the event that stands out in the past that can be seen with due perspective, and this event alone possesses the force that will carry it to the heart. The argument that the commonplace events and scenes of to-day should be used to teach love of home and familiar things may be well enough for other arts, but it does not apply to pageantry.

Another principle of good pageantry is that it should be native to the place in which it is presented. And it should be constructive of the society that presents it. In fact there is little justification for pageantry except as it serves these ends. A pageant referring to unfamiliar and distant places becomes a mere show. The ceremonies which were rich in social significance become but the evolutions and manipulations of sensational display. And while ceremony is the material of pageantry it is not the end. The end is the representation of the large truths of social life through the past costuming of that life in episode and manner and dress. The truth will never be seen through the ceremony save in those cases in which the answering spirit is found in the audience. It is only the native pageant that is a real pageant.

In all the principles above suggested there is involved the further one that the pageant is more an art

is in drama. It is true that the unity of the pageant is not as explicit as is that of the play. In the play the unity is one not only of theme, but of plot and treatment. This is not necessarily the case in the pageant. The greatest diversity in method and in plot is acceptable as long as the unity of theme is kept intact. This unity is usually the outgrowth of the inherent solidity and congruity of the historic materials presented.

All idea of unity of time is, of course, dismissed from the pageant. But every pageant depends upon a clear time-schedule which of itself provides some sense of time-unity. It is difficult to imagine a pageant in which the different scenes do not represent successive episodes in a chain of history. In a sense quite unlike that in which the term was used in the time of Elizabeth, the pageant is a "progress"; that is, it deals with successive events in the march of civilization. And there is no arbitrary limit to the amount of time that may be suggested in the process of the pageant. Parker's Warwick Pageant covers the time from the Druids to the seventeenth century. The Mid-Gloucestershire Pageant of England had still greater scope and brought the pageant down to modern times over a period of twenty-one centuries.

Now, these pageants are no less unified than are those which cover a shorter period. There must be recognized, however, the tendency in all art to gather itself together by the manipulation of the materials in such a way that a large outlook is seen through a narrow opening. This tendency has been seen in the pageant. Indeed, it was this tendency which in the history of the drama brought an end to pageant art and substituted the more closely knit art of the theatre. Already the tendency is seen not only to narrow the scope of the pageant, but to draw its action together in such a way that there is connection between the episodes. This is the method of the chronicle play. A striking illustration of this tendency is found in Mr. John Steven McGroarty's Mission Play of San Gabriel, California. Here there is a true pageant which is at the same time something of a historical chronicle. This pageant represents the history of the district through authentic episodes, and attaches to these the dances, the songs, and ceremonies which are the *divertissement* of the action. And the entire movement is compressed within the limit of sixty-five years. By this means a complete pageant is made to centre around the life and spiritual influence of one man, Father Serrá, the spiritual father of Lower California. The tendency here seen is found in less clearly marked forms in many of the best recent pageants.

Though the pageant may cover a long period of time there is one law that it cannot afford to ignore. This is the law of the economy of the attention of the audience. No pageant should demand much more than two hours in the presentation. Anything more than that is given under handicap. The same law restricts the number of episodes that can profitably be presented. Naturally, no arbitrary number can be given. A large pageant which is constructed of dumb shows and ceremonies may present more episodes than a smaller pageant in which more dramatic and expository action is presented. In the former type there may be twenty or more episodes. In the latter it is seldom advisable to present more than eight. The advantage of the latter type in clarity and force may be readily seen.

This brings us to another vital problem of structure of the pageant, the kinds of action of which the pageant is made. A study of pageant structure shows us that the pageant is made up of two separate plots. The first may be called the "salient plot"; and the second may be called the "contributory plot."

The salient plot of the pageant is composed of all the material, usually of a historic nature, of the episodes themselves. These episodes are "dramatic moments," or, as some one has said, "distillations" of the spirit of a historic event. Usually these episodes are spoken; often they are acted in dumb show or in mass actions; sometimes they are given in the form of tableaux and spectacular arrangements. It is on this structure of the pageant that historic scholarship should be expended. In heraldry, in costume, in historic detail, even in language, these should be carefully studied and authentic. The English pageant masters have been very careful to secure accuracy in this material. For the armory and heraldry of their pageants they usually employ antiquarians and county heralds. The "Historical Notes to the York Pageant," covering matters of heraldry, weapons, and historic documents made a book of seventy-six pages.

Aside from the salient plot there is the contributory plot, and this must be clearly distinguished from the salient plot. The contributory plot, or, as it may be called, the "containing plot," is comprised of all the actions which are necessary to explain and unite the main plot into a coherent whole. The contributory plot is composed of prologue and epilogue, link passages, explanatory and narrative passages, and interludes. The convention of the containing plot has not been worked out in modern times. We have in our catalogues of theatric expedients no chorus that can be accepted without question. Therefore, it lies pretty much with the ingenuity of the director how he will treat his plot.

The first purpose of the contributory plot is to make the action clear by prior explanations of episodes and by linking up the connections. The instrument that may be used in serving this end varies with different pageants. Some pageant masters use the chorus as does Parker in his Warwick Pageant, when he creates a Druid Chorus. Other expedients are that of a herald, a man-at-arms, and a town crier.

After the contributory plot has served the purpose of explanation it has the further purpose of elevating and magnifying the action. It does this by suggesting the larger meanings, the atmosphere of sentiment or heroism through which the scene should be viewed. For these purposes it can call to its aid symbolic dancing, the beauties of verse and elocution, the spiritual claims of allegory. But care should be taken to make the contributory plot truly contributory. If this action becomes more important than the salient action, the whole nature of the pageant is vitiated.

On this a word of warning is required. It is that too much care cannot be taken to keep the two plots distinct, and to subordinate the minor to the major plot. There is a growing custom among many American pageant masters to mingle in the salient plot imaginative materials which belong, if they should exist at all, in the containing plot. Sometimes an entire allegorical episode is introduced in an attempt to symbolize vague movements or spirits, such as War, Education, Progress; sometimes it is the personification of spirits of nature, Health, Fruitfulness, or such natural objects as the local mountain, the river, or woods.

These are sometimes represented by young dancers who mingle more or less closely in the concrete action, influencing it to one or another outcome. Effective as this may seem at first glance, it is a mixing of values that can lead only to the downfall of pageantry as an art. Nothing is gained by this custom but the confusion of two different methods of presentation and the consequent compromising of both.

If something is needed to break the dull detail of

the authentic record, the contributary plot provides ample scope. In this the English pageant masters, who are always strict in their code, have pointed a way. If the realistic episodes promise to be too unrelieved, they introduce a full masque in the middle of the action of the pageant, but separated from it. For the Oxford Pageant, Professor Walter Raleigh wrote a "Masque of the Mediæval Curriculum," which was introduced between the sixth and seventh episodes, and in the Chelsea Pageant of 1908 there was introduced a children's masque of "The Faerie Queene."

The care taken in keeping the pageant true to type in symbolism and allegory should also be shown in the handling of music and dancing. And this requires a firm hand in the pageant master both for the reason that these arts are very tempting through their easy appeal to the audience, and also because those in charge of these features are likely to press their claims. Music and dancing are excellent in their place, and may even be introduced into the body of the salient action. But when this is done it should be clear that they are associated with the plot. Music, dances, and folk-lore elements when introduced should be justified by the action itself. Thus, in the Warwick Pageant dances and fêtes are introduced as before Queen Elizabeth. The judicious are made to grieve when a dance is introduced to interpret symbolically a concrete action, or when a lyrical narrative is introduced amidst the action to tell what is going on. For the dance does not interpret nor does the lyric narrate. It is the use of the vague abstract to serve the clear concrete, the weighing-down of the music and dancing with meaning that is a clog to its freedom.

This is not a book of instructions to pageant masters on the staging of the pageant. No attention is given to such matters as the choice of committees, the assignment of tasks, the choice of costumes, the laying-out of the ground, the selection and training of the actors, for the reason that these are things that are learned by doing rather than precept. There are, however, some matters connected with the staging of the pageant on which precept may not be amiss.

First, as to the position of the pageant stage there are some simple considerations. If, as is probable, we are to accept the dramatic type of pageant, the choice of a stage is an important item. We often hear of pageants, which required the coöperative work of hundreds of people through weeks of time, going to waste on account of a poor stage location. The principles upon which the stage should be selected are two: First, that it should provide proper audience accommodations; second, that it should possess a proper background. If the pageant is to satisfy its purposes at all, the first consideration of location is that it shall be clearly within sight of the audience. This in fact demands a slight incline sloping down to the stage, as pageant crowds are usually so large that it is inadvisable to build grandstands or bleachers of any height.

The background of the pageant stage comes second in importance to the audience slope. Directors have been known to place their performances on the slope of a hill above their audience on the plea that the background justified the position. Of what value a background would be to a pageant that could not be seen was perhaps not considered. But given a proper audience room the background is exceedingly important to the success of the pageant. The pageant is not a circus or a fair and should not be placed in the midst of an open field with audience on all sides. A clean-cut background, whether of building or trees and hills, is of great value in emphasizing the unity of the pageant. The background of old buildings and ruins, as of Warwick Castle, and the background of distant river and mountains, as at Quebec, were so adequate that they were indeed a part of the pageant.

There are a few principles of scenery which can be summarized. First, whatever the background, whether of nature or buildings, use it to its fullest effectiveness for all scenes. Second, avoid as far as possible the necessity of erecting scenery for separate episodes. When the background needs supplementing, erect battlements and buildings of an ambiguous type as was done for the Oxford Pageant. Third, as far as possible make scenery immovable and use it for different purposes. The writer is convinced that realistic painted scenery is a drawback to the pageant.

THE PAGEANT IN AMERICA

It is unnecessary to enlarge on the social uses of the pageant. As an awakener of social spirit and community coöperation the pageant is well appreciated. Let any one who is unaware of this look through the indexes to current periodicals for references to the pageant. All over the country the pageant is actively showing the sweetness and reality of village life, the richness and dignity of our yesterdays. It is calling people back from vague discontent to the discovery of the wealth at their own doors. It is uncovering the mementoes of the past, and ransacking attics for the costumes, the spinning-wheels, the furniture, the old shawls and lace of our mothers and grandmothers. It is serving the cause of the homely virtues and the healthy sentiments. More than that, it is extending a hand of brotherhood across the world. Sherborne, Oxford, Warwick, York all made room in their ceremonies for towns of the same name the world over.

Naturally, such an instrument as this does not pass unnoticed by those who have a programme to promulgate. Already people are using it to establish a number of cases from the right of women to the vote to the necessity of "swatting the fly." And for these purposes the pageant serves effectively and well, although now and then it is seen almost to break under the burden of its earnest message of self-conscious betterment. When put to its best use it is always ready to fill a social gap, to serve as a high social substitute for lower social activities, to engage a leisure hour, and to give expression and direction to the wayward impulses of a newly awakened society.

There is no doubt that we in America have not the rich background for pageantry that Great Britain can show. Our pageants cannot go back to Cæsar or Cymbeline. Naturally, this fact has an influence on the type of pageantry presented in this country. Lacking the ordered and more cultivated stretches of history of older countries, our writers of pageant are called upon themselves to isolate the stimulating moments of a history that was largely one of hardships and pioneering rather than one of ceremonies. In the rather drab background of our history the Indian legends, and the shifting civilizations of the red man and the whites, the Spaniards, the French, and the Anglo-Saxons, present the four touches of real color. But it is real color, and the pageant-maker has not yet mixed his materials in such a way as to suggest its possibilities.

Too easily assuming a lack of glories in the past, some directors are centring their attention in the present and throwing into high relief the wonders of present "achievement." Any such glorification of the present must come with a bad grace. And with even poorer grace comes the custom of some of presenting the past as a crude and shameful background for "present enlightenment and progress." Aside from the bad taste of this attitude it is quite lacking in truthful perspective. Without reverence there can be no art. And in self-vaunting there can be neither art nor social welfare. The good pageant is one that strives to make us worthy of our yesterdays by enriching their promise.

We have seen evidences of the broad distribution of the pageant, its genuinely social quality, its fidelity to many of the principles of primitive art. It remains now only to say that all indications show that the pageant is not a fixed but a tentative art form, that it represents one stage in the development from the lowest to the higher forms of dramatic expression. This is shown both by its history and by its inherent character. Historically the pageant has always appeared early in the development of national drama. It arose after the rude and disconnected ceremonies of the religious or folk festival had been gathered to focus in one action. It represented the external drama of the nation or the province. It satisfied the broader motives of national feeling, but it gave no scope to the study of the inner motives of men or the revelation of their secret souls and their higher yearnings. Historically the pageant form has always given way to the stricter forms of drama in which motives count more than actions, and spirit than flesh. The structure of the modern pageant confirms this. This pageant has already accomplished much in providing work for idle hands, in drawing together many people in the service of beauty. It has done much to discover the broad and palpable facts of our national backgrounds of nature and history. But already its limitations are becoming apparent. When one desires to express a more spiritual message he finds the pageant inert and helpless. From it he then tends to turn to other forms of dramatic art in which his meaning may be more appropriately bodied forth. And then he turns to the masque or the formal drama. The best thing that the pageant can do is to create its own place in the heart of America and then give way to other forms. The best mark of its success will be that it compels the demand for the service of other higher forms and so renders itself unnecessary. And apparently this is the process that is taking place. Those who are looking for an American drama will not fail to note this portent.

CHAPTER VI

THE PROMISE OF AN AMERICAN DRAMA

IN our study thus far we have continually used the terms "American" and "American drama" without making any effort to define the one or locate the other. And yet in these two terms there lies whatever significance there may be found in this book. For if, as many think, the term "American" has not yet achieved a connotation of its own, then indeed our drama cannot yet be defined. If, furthermore, and this we hold to be the case, drama itself may serve as an instrument by which the meaning of America may be realized, then our problem resolves itself into an immediate study of the promise of dramatic art as an exponent of American life and spirit. To introduce this study three questions may be appropriate: First, What steps, if any, have been taken toward the achievement of a distinctively American drama? Second, What is the promise of their early success? Third, What form will the drama take when it appears, if appear it does?

Now, answers to these questions have been implied in much that has been said in these pages. It will be our purpose in this chapter to sum up what has gone before and give it a particular focus. In answer to the first question, it may be said that American society is now very active in measures that should lead toward an American drama. In this there is implied the answer to the second question, which is that many processes which have been at work for a long time, and other processes which are now beginning, seem to promise a not far distant consummation in a dramatic art of the twentieth century. And in answer to the third question, it must be said, how tritely the author is aware, that we can look for the substance and form of the American play only in the substance and form of American life. There are no laws for art other than the laws by which men govern themselves, and there is no material of dramatic art other than the substance of mankind.

THE NEW ORGANIZATION OF THE AMERICAN THEATRE

In speaking of the coming American play we need to be careful to emphasize an idea that has all along been implied in this book. That is, that the dramatic art of a period is made up not alone of the plays that are presented, but of the entire institution of the theatre of the time, comprising its actors, its producers, its managers, its agents, its many artists and workers, as well as its writers. The drama of the time is the whole institution of the stage of the time. In looking forward to an American drama, therefore, we cannot limit ourselves to the play itself. We cannot even consider this first. Before we can consider the play we must study the machinery upon which rests the relationship between the play and its audience. The drama is quite as much a matter of organization as it is of art composition. The promise of American drama lies, as a matter of fact, as much in reorganization as in new forms of playwriting, and no less in new methods of business than in new principles of art.

It may be said that a healthy and normal organization of the theatre, an organization that adapts itself to the social life of the people in a direct way, is the first prerequisite of dramatic art. To the extent that America differs from other nations in social constitution, in geographical distribution, and political ideals, its organization of the art of the theatre should differ from that of other nations. We may learn much on theatrical organization from the systems of the Continent, but what we learn should be in matters of principles rather than of methods. In the end the problem of theatrical organization must be solved by Americans in the American way. It is a comparatively late discovery, and one that still requires some courage in its application, that the strongly marked characteristics of a nation are always its opportunities in art rather than its drawbacks. The trouble with our artists has been that they have attempted to impose on America artistic codes and systems that have been borrowed from other countries. Because they have been unable to do so they have bewailed our unreadiness for art. The time is coming when American life itself will provide our materials and American standards will supply our form as well in organization as in technique. Then only shall we be able to speak of an American art of the theatre.

American drama has been seriously hampered by the fact that the organization upon which the drama depends and from which it draws its support is un-American and is not directed to the needs of the American people. I am not now referring to the nationality of the business men of the theatre, for this is of no consequence. Nor do I question that the organization of the theatre has paralleled the organization of other big business in centralization and system of distribution. But it is greatly to be questioned whether the American manager has shown the keen knowledge of his wares, the shrewd insight into the demands of his patronage, that have characterized the national distributors in other lines of merchandise. For one thing the American theatre has been organized on the basis of an imported rather than a domestic art. New York, which is the centre of theatre organization, is theatrically much nearer Europe than it is to the rest of the country. And the organization of the theatre was based upon the principle of an importing institution, with headquarters at the seaboard, and distributing offices scattered over the country. The man at the head of the institution did not know his wares and did not know his audiences. He was innocent of any conception of the fact that in an art there should always be maintained a close relationship between the source of supply and the consumer. The result has been the establishment of a single un-American centre of judgment for American plays which has dominated the playwright to his hurt and alienated the consumers of the nation. In an art, the very life of which depends upon a close intimacy with the life of society, such a system of organization is fatal. And the problem is intensified by the broad area of the country and its diversity of sectional point of view.

Most of the suggestions which have been made for the reorganization of the American theatre are in their way as faulty as the organization they would attempt to displace. Building on the theory of the Comédie Française, men have argued for a National American Theatre in Washington or Chicago which should in these centres draw together the best standards of the nation in one high focus. Such a suggestion is futile. Leaving out of consideration the fact that the Comédie Française was established under a different régime from that of the present, and now very imperfectly serves France, there remains the further fact that the United States is far larger in area than France and very much more diversified in social and race character. No single national theatre could ever live *as such* in this country for two years. If it survived, it would be as a local institution of high standard, supported by

the community, and serviceable at a distance only as
an indirect influence.

Another suggestion often made is based upon the
system of Germany. It is that the separate States or
municipalities should establish and support by state
grant subsidized theatres to serve the local community in which they are placed. Though this comes far
nearer reason than the former scheme, it, too, is pro-
pounded with little reference to our system of society.
The State is neither ready nor is it able under our
codes to support a state theatre upon a basis worthy
of consideration. If it is to be a theatre for the many,
there is no need of state interference; and a theatre
for the few could hardly claim state support. Both
artistically and financially the state theatre might exchange for the evils we have evils that are quite as
serious. And little is to be expected from subsidy by
private beneficence. There would be in this some encouragement to experiment, and some support of the
art in its unproductive years, but the necessary thing,
without which we shall never have a theatre of our
own, the immediate contact with the life and organization of the people, would be lacking. In the end it
will be from the people themselves, and the people
alone, that the art will come.

Though the two revolutionary suggestions that are
based on old-world models seem hardly to promise improvement in American theatrical organization, we
need not necessarily despair of change for the better.

For if we turn our eyes from Europe to our own country, we shall find at home, working out of the processes of our society, new forms of organization that are far in advance of any that have hitherto been tried. A survey of present conditions and future promise in America shows some interesting developments that are not without their elements of hope.

In the first place, we see now that the syndicate system has all along contained the germs of its own undoing. The syndicate system has not been the success that its friends and most fearful opponents supposed it to be. It was too unwieldy. The district it had to cover was too large. And there never was and never could be complete monopoly in the hands of one person or set of persons. The system came very near to monopoly, but it always contained an element of the unmanageable, which was unsatisfied local interest. This local interest has effectually weakened the syndicate by striking a blow at the whole system of theatrical organization in America of the present. For years the syndicate existed by adroitly compromising with new masterful figures that arose in Portland, Los Angeles, Chicago, and Syracuse. Its power was therefore no power. It was a semblance of power based upon successive compromise. And in the end the syndicate came to be but a name. Ruled from New York, and out of touch with the provinces, it was doomed from the start by the vitality of local interests. And to-day these local interests are becoming stronger every hour, and the fact that strong men were soon placated and organized into the system does not vitiate at all the fact of their power or the significance of its sources. These men were significant not because they beat the syndicate on its own ground, but because they beat the syndicate on their own ground. They showed that the ultimate power of the future lies in the local circuit, supported from a centre and created from the life of a district. That a district will support its own theatres irrespective of New York has now been clearly established in experience. The significance of this fact for a coming American drama can only be suggested.

Incident to the gradual loosening of power of the syndicate there has proceeded the gradual strengthening of the movements for local theatres. This has not applied to the professional organization of the theatre. It is too late to restore the fortunes of those theatres from which the life was sapped by the extra-territorial control. The movement had to be one altogether of reconstruction. As a rule this is a movement from outside the theatre. It is participated in by thousands of men and women who see that the theatre has failed of its opportunity, and in the amateur and professional field are determined to bring the theatre back to a closer touch with the life of the district. It has, indeed, been fortunate that the movement has come apart from the theatre, that it has secured little from the established institution of the stage, for it has called into the service of social amusement and art thousands of men and women of vision who in other times have been alienated from the stage. The number of these local theatre movements is legion. The local theatre movements of Boston, Philadelphia, Chicago, Milwaukee, Madison; the work of producing societies such as the Wisconsin Dramatic Society, the Chicago Theatre Society, Donald Robertson's Players, the Drama Society of New York, the Stage Society of New York; the work of the open-air theatre producers of Point Loma, Berkeley, the Harvard Stadium, and Carmel by the Sea; the work of the Little Country Theatre; the noteworthy achievement of the Bohemian Club of California, all point to the leavening of the mass by new principles of organization outside the established theatre. These are being aided by the colleges, which are studying organization as a feature of the problem of dramatic art, and are serving as busy producing centres, and by the inauguration of the Carnegie School of Drama at Pittsburg, which is supplying a new model of organization of a theatre in connection with an established institution.

The best of this movement is that it does not end with merely leavening the social lump. The first necessity these local theatres face is that of finding plays, adequate in standard and appropriate in length and character. Whether organized to support the new drama or not, these local companies are soon led to the use of original plays. Often they begin with the newest thing in the English and Continental field, and from these go by gradual stages to the presentation of plays of the province. And this is in truth and strict honor the destiny of such societies. They are not even attacking their problem unless they undertake frankly and fairly the production of American plays. I think of the words of Donald Robertson, who will be honored as the beginner of much that is now coming to pass. He said, "The justification of a repertory theatre is to play its own plays and to go for inspiration to the masters." It is no mere matter of policy, this production of home plays. It is a matter of the life of the institution and the honesty of its spirit. One should not need to argue against the borrowed or transplanted spirit. The simple fact is that there is no borrowed or transplanted spirit. The spirit either lives or it dies, and it lives only in its own habitat. The trouble with our drama in the past has been that it has been an errant drama, without home, without roots, without soil. There is no wonder that it soon lost its life.

The living play must be presented by an institution which itself lives in the social life of the district. This the theatre has forgotten; and society has therefore left the theatre, and has proceeded to nurture new organisms outside the theatre. And these organisms will fail of their purpose if they fail to flower in American plays. Those who feel the full strength of this truth are often counseled to hesitate on account of the necessary crudity of the play in an early period of its development. The American play of the present, it is said, is far behind the better standards of taste of the American people. A critic who argues in this way fails to value deeply enough the essential qualities of a piece of art, that it be sincere and not self-conscious. Given these qualities and others may follow. Violate them, and no amount of dexterity and technique will save the play. No plea of the greater skill or artistry of the foreign play should be permitted to induce a manager to give all his place to plays from other lands. The task now is to discover the genuine American play, and theatres may indeed be judged for their virility, courage, and social value by their fidelity to the American standard. Naturally, this is the more difficult task, for it lacks the aids of foreign judgments. But it is the task that will bring the greater reward. In spite of its difficulty it is the task that the little theatres, the local experimental theatres, are called upon to do. They are particularly qualified to do it, for they have neither traditions to uphold nor dividends to pay. Upon their assumption of the task will depend the place they will take in the future history of the American theatre.

THE PRELIMINARY FORMS OF AMERICAN DRAMA

In another respect, quite apart from systems of organization, there seems to be on the way a movement for the American motive in dramatic art. This is in the spontaneous development during the last ten years of the system of social festival, pageantry, and masque. The importance of this movement from the point of view of dramatic art is very great. The movement begins not as art, but as spontaneous social activity. It is the outgrowth of newly released powers seeking avenues of expression. It is valuable as a utilization of the leisure hours of city people. It means the spirit of health finding constructive means to combat the insidious dangers of the wasted hour. The festival, whether on the village green, in the city park, on the campus of the college, or in the crowded settlement, is corrective and creative. By the terms of its existence, it must be built of the substance of its surroundings. It is composed of episodes from the lore of the folk comprising the district. It is subject to no trammels of organization or precedent. Indeed, it is often without organization, or it provides its own organization out of the instruments at hand. Herein lies a great portion of the significance of the festival movement and its promise for a future American drama. It utilizes the machinery of the school, the church, the settlement, the club, and brings dramatic art back to the sources from which it has always sprung, the social life of the people. It connects itself with their interests, and is governed by their forms. Its rules are derived from the rules by which they live, and its spirit is their spirit. Drama and amusement alike have long forgotten this truth, and so they have become alienated from the interests and the support of the people.

In this, too, there is found much of the significance of educational dramatics and the dramatics of propaganda. People have discovered that this art, which was formerly altogether out of their hands, really belongs to them, that it is made of their substance, supported by their life, and that it dies when they desert it. They have lost their contempt for the amateur, their mystic veneration of the professional, their many illusions as to the stage, illusions that it was the care of the artificial theatre to foster, and they have taken dramatic activities part and total back into their own hands. They have ceased to be auditors and have become participants, ceased to be recipients and have become givers, ceased to be the exploited and have begun to use the drama in its manifold forms, for the education of their youth, for the exposition of their problems, for the expression of their lives, and for the lightening of their leisure hour. That no great play has as yet come is no indication that this movement has failed, or that this readoption of the theatre by the people has done other than provide a clear road of progress for the genuine drama of the future.

So far we have loosely referred to the festival and the social play hour as dramatic. They are in fact only dramatic in tendency. But movements flower rapidly under the processes of these days. "First the corn, then the ear, then the full blade in the ear." And men now living may see the full blade grow from the corn. The festivals of the social leisure hour are already taking on a form that parallels the forms of drama when the art was young. In the chapter on the pageant it was shown that the pageant had developed in a decade to an important place in the social and art status of the nation. The pageant is the outgrowth of that settling movement, that tendency to form and certainty, to unity and expressiveness, that always follows hard on any vital revolution. The pageant is an artistic settling of social values. It is crude as yet, no doubt, yet even in its crude form is governed by the principles that conduce to a fresh and expressive art. The pageant is made of the life of the people, it is formed by themselves, it deals objectively and not profoundly with the externals of their lives, it respects the past and builds upon it, it venerates the future and prepares for it. It is common, democratic, universal, not too subtle, yet capable of a strong and dignified beauty, a clear and trumpet message. The pageant is not a self-conscious art form. It is made up largely of play. It is American because it permits the use of the many, it harmonizes the different kinds, and it gives no place to the sickly, the sentimental, or the introspective.

But a step beyond the pageant has been taken. This has been done according to that native principle of self help and self-expression by which all problems are solved and all heights are scaled. After the external comes the internal; after the show comes the message. After the accidental beauty of substance comes the purposed beauty of form, the skilled manipulation of all machinery to the depiction of the rarer zones of the spirit. The masque as an American thing springs out of the conditions of our civilization, but rises above them to a purer expression of our national spirit. In it the poignancy of our contests, the pathos of our defeats, and the glories of our victories, have already found sporadic appearance. No less American than the pageant, but more universal, the masque is coming to give new interpretation to those aspects of our life which in our hurry of living we have heretofore passed by, the secret springs of social conscience, the stern inspiration of duty and justice, the subtle call of beauty in common things. And with the masque will come the artist. The festival and the pageant still show something of the charm of the unstudied and the spontaneous. They are good because they are true; and they are true because they are ourselves. But they do not call for that unique contribution, without which there is no living art, the creative touch of the poet. For it is the poet who provides the one thing necessary to a living art, the vision of genius, the outlook upon immensity. His is the alembic of the final beauty. Let the poets of the nation once see their opportunity, let the pageant but plough the soil, and there will appear in new forms, not yet dreamed of, utilizing the powers of electricity, of invention, of music, of the aeroplane, creative poetic concepts welded of all the arts and illuminating the harmony of our American life. The promise is at hand. It has even, here and there, as at St. Louis, found magnificent expression. The soil is now being tilled by those who go before.

One healthy thing about the whole movement for a remade American drama is that it is beginning outdoors. The drama always begins outdoors. It takes to roofs and houses only after the spirit has surrendered to the formula. And lusty drama always has something of outdoors about it. Only the extreme codes of the comedy of manners and clinical naturalism depend upon the convention of an inclosed place. The Greek tragedians and comedians, Plautus and Terence, Shakespeare and Hans Sachs, Calderon and Lope de Vega, Goldoni and the *Commedia del' Arte*, the Chinese drama and the new drama of South America, all have something of the open air about them. Their *rencontres* are usually in the open or in common meeting-places. One might easily push this too far, and it is not a rock upon which one would care to break an argument. But it is certain that in the same degree that the lamp and the study are dangerous to art the open air is happy for art. Whether, as in Italy and Spain, the climate is adapted to open-air performances, or, as in England, it offers little security, the beginnings of the drama are in either case under the sky. And it is not stretching the imagination too far to think that the beginnings of American drama will be in the open air. Whatever we may think of the value of our contribution to civilization, we know that the heart of America is in its outdoors. The conquests of America have been open-air conquests. The typical American is the pioneer. Our urban types are not yet developed, nor will they have provided differentiated groups for many years. And for such types as we have for the city the world has already created a drama better than any we can create by imitation. How futile to turn away from the veritable impression of our American life, with its sense of vast reaches of territory, its alternating stretches of prairie, mountain, and forest, for a transplanted city sophistication. Not the city man, but the pioneer, the lumberman, the villager, are the true types of American life. All unknown to us, these figures have found their way into the first form of our dramatic art. In so doing they have represented that eternal tendency by which life begins always under the sun.

AMERICA AND HER PROVINCES

Are we, then, to believe that the present organization of the theatre is to be altogether displaced? By no means. Only those artificial features of the theatre that fail to adjust themselves to the necessities of the time will be discarded. The general structure of theatrical organization, that goes back to Cibber and Garrick and Boucicault, will still be found useful. Of

all social institutions the theatre is most flexible. And
it will be through pressure from without, by appropriation into the professional and commercial system of
the best features of the present experimental drama,
that the organization of the theatre will learn its new
function.

There are some lessons the theatre will undoubtedly
learn. Chief among these will be the lesson that the organization of the American theatre must regard the
facts of the American status, as distinguished from the
status of the foreign countries, England particularly,
from which its methods have been drawn. The geographical problem in America varies widely from that
in England. An organization that will serve perfectly
for the compact islands of Britain would be hopelessly
inefficient in the wider expanse of our territory. Yet we
have tried to control our provincial theatre from the
capital in New York in the way they have managed
the British theatre from London. If England is becoming weary of the overlordship of London, how
much more must we in America be weary of the theatrical control of New York. One may reach any portion of the British Isles within twenty hours of London. When a play goes to Seattle from New York, it
is almost a week away from its centre. That New
York does not satisfy the Pacific Slope is indicated by
the fact that it is here that the system of local management is strongest. From the point of view of mere
business acumen it is surprising that the business men

of the theatre have not seen that the centre of management of the theatre should be somewhat near the centre of patronage. Those business men who have made fortunes out of the theatre have been those who have organized their own circuits, or those who have engaged in the vaudeville and motion-picture business, which, as we have seen, are more rationally organized than the legitimate theatre. Some few have dared to fight for their right to create local stock companies and provincial chains of theatres. These it is of whom New York has had to become afraid. At heart drama must always be an art rather than a business, but the status of the business is not a bad index to the health of the art. The business of the theatre has not been good business for many years. It may not be a bad day for American drama when the local business man sees the opportunity of the theatre and determines that at least a fair share of the increment shall remain at home.

More telling than the business argument is the social argument for the reorganization of our theatre. This depends upon the recognition that our country is not one homogeneous whole, but is an aggregation of separate units each one of which has some solidity in itself. For there is such a thing as provincial spirit. This is quite another thing from parochialism. It is a compound of many forces. Among these are the common heritage of race of many who settled in the same part of the country, a certain uniformity of calling or activity involved in the residence in the same district, and that undeniable thing called "local feeling," in which climate, natural objects, and character of life all have their share. One does not need to go as far as the widely disparate attitudes of the South and North to find this distinction based upon locality. It is found between New York and California; and among neighbors of closer residence it is found between California and Washington, Massachusetts and Maine, Wisconsin and Indiana. Kansas has an atmosphere, a temper of her own, unlike any other. Pennsylvania could not possibly be mistaken for Colorado, Idaho for Minnesota. These distinctions go back to forces that are as strong as life itself, for they are the forces that form and make life. And it is particularly these explicit distinctions that give drama its opportunity as art. It is the business of the dramatist to discover these and to use them, to raise them to symbolic value as revelations of the essential characteristics of social life.

It seems hardly necessary to explain that, in speaking for provincialism as an instrument by which the concrete truths of life are grasped, one has no intention of questioning the force of the large social units of the nation and the race. It is the belief that the larger units may best be grasped and apprehended by means of the smaller unit. But in this there is not and there could not be any denial of the larger unit. The whole is not made smaller when the part is apprehended. In seeing the district clearly we do no injustice to the nation. Social thinkers have long since discarded the view that strength lies in mere uniformity, or that a repetition of the typical brings stability. National life may better be compared with an orchestra than with the multiplied music of one instrument. The thing that gives power to a nation is that architectonic quality which comes from the fit arrangement of the parts in a stable and lofty whole. There is no disparagement of America as a whole when we ask that drama help to discover America through the medium of her provinces. There is rather a recognition of that large disinterestedness which is the nation itself, that free comprehensiveness that lies outside the power of any particular plea, that comprises all strains and all tempers, and is subject to the control of none, that rules with the benignity of a great idea over the many participating groups. The drama of the district will never be untrue to the national life, for the national life is always implied in the district.

One of the chief traits of American character, both individually and nationally, is an easy assumption of power. In words we are braggart enough. But in deeds we seldom put out our full energy, for we are seldom called upon to do so. And since there has not been the necessity we are not even conscious of what our strength may be. Assuming that it is ample, we proceed with what we have to do. And while in words we are braggarts, in our actions we are modest. The result is that we are not conscious of the significance

of the things that are being done. Great deeds are
done quietly, and almost in a rough-and-ready way.
Our style has not caught up with our substance. Our
ceremonies are not yet equivalent to our dignities.
And so we have not yet been greatly deluded with
pride of the factitious. We are not willing to put out
much on merely making a show. Now, this is not
humility, or boorishness; perhaps it is a good-natured
and a little awkward unconcern. Not having to draw
on the complete reserves of our power, we have not
measured its amount. Power is handled easily because it is not recognized as power. Particularly there
is lacking the "sense" of power that comes from
nicely arranged hierarchies of potentates. When
power is limited and administered, it becomes a serious thing. But the American sense of humor, crude as
it is, and the American "common sense" are our best
attributes. It will be a bad day when we lose them,
for then we shall have lost our security of unconcern. We shall become afraid, and grow watchful and
take on manners. American common sense punctures
many an affectation, not only for the other man, but
for the American himself.

If we only knew it, these are happy days in our national life. We are most happy and most ourselves in
our lack of that nationality which other nations have
achieved and which we must recognize as the stamp of
their decline. We shall be most fortunate if we can
keep our strength potential. We do not care to make

it actual. In spite of strong temptation we have not deluded ourselves with the cult of effective armament, nor have we held to the illusion of the necessity of sin to high civilization. We hate sin in quite a bigoted and middle-class and bland way. Everything points to the fact that America has not yet been discovered. America to-day is a great brooding abstraction. And it is best for us and for the world that it be so. For by this America is permitted to stand for the Idea, quite frankly, quite concretely, quite securely, and — best of all — quite unafraid of facts. There are no facts that she needs to fear as long as she broods in the undiscovered power and unbroken peace of the Idea. Under her wings are her separate districts, very sure of themselves, hard at work, self-realizing, like the ancient city-states. Something will be lost that can never be recovered when America as a whole means anything as concrete as they.

Well, while America is but a majestic abstraction, why look for an art that will express her directly? As America herself looks to her provinces for the word of authority that will represent her separate services, to Pittsburg, to the forests, to the prairies, to the mining States, to the Pacific Slope, for their contribution of inventive genius, business organization, muscular men, radical ideas, chivalric sentiments, and impulses toward art, so let the drama achieve the expression of the larger America through the province. Thus will the themes of American drama be diversified, and the meaning of the term "American" be revealed in richer and subtler form.

What are some of the themes that will be laid upon dramatic art? One thing is certain, dramatic art will come home. By this we mean that the drama will treat not the fixed and crude types of an outworn art that misrepresented a past society, but the real experiences of men and women, the veritable fortunes of their lives, the adjustments they have had to make to a civilization that has rapidly changed front. So far from saying that we can have no literature until we have achieved a national type, it would be more true to say that it is precisely at this period that a literature should be expected to come. Art is in demand in periods of preparation, therefore in periods of incompleteness. When a nation has achieved its type, it has lost the need, as it has lost the lure, of art. The service art renders is that of self-discovery and self-expression. It is therefore precisely to-day that we should be looking for our literature and drama, because we are in process of preparation, we are seeking and finding.

Appropriately enough, since literature is the voice of the search rather than of the achievement, the song of the gleam rather than of the fixed light, it is in these themes of preparation that we find the strongest and best materials of a new art. The new art finds itself in the social discovery. Its experiments are but reflexes of the social readjustments, the mental queries and replies by which another order is established. With this type of subject-matter our life is rich to-day. We are becoming conscious in our political thinking of something immediate and differentiating, that raises us in some relief from the rest of the world. From such consciousness the new art will come.

THE THEMES OF AMERICAN DRAMA

Among the many fields that lie open to the dramatist four come to mind. All of these are typically American. They deal with the as yet unsolved problems of our society — problems that may never be solved, but may, as such problems do, melt away into other problems more pregnant for later days. All of them contain in little the tragedies and comedies that are reflections of larger significations. The first of these fields is that of the race borderland between the Indian and the white man. Civilization has seldom if ever shown such a dramatic juxtaposition of diverse races as that presented by the conquering push of the white man over the hunting-grounds of the red. It was no mere case of survival of the fittest, no struggle between the Roman and the Hun. On the one side was a simple people, too imaginative, too simple, too native-true, to be called savages, both by their virtues and their weaknesses ill-prepared to fight the battle of survival against a stronger foe. On the other side was the white man, trained for conquest by a thousand years of city-building and sophistication, pioneers by thought, woodsmen by intention, fighters by the cold and cruel pressure of moral foresight and power to wait. They won by knowing that destiny was on the side of the immaterial rather than of the material forces. It was not the Indians that were killed who mark the tragedy. The tragedy came from the clash of two points of view and the suffocation of the simpler. That the outcome was inevitable makes the tragedy no less acute. The Indian was lost in a miasma of thought he could not fathom, of a civilization he was unprepared for. All his best blows fell harmless against a breastplate of alien intelligence he was never able to pierce.

Here is material for the dramatist, indeed, material that will open doors to truth. But of this material we have in our drama next to nothing. A century ago Chateaubriand found some of its romantic meaning, the paradox of values, so to speak, by which civilization was the new Hun, that came down and harried to extinction a simple Utopia of unspoiled nature. But Chateaubriand's Indian is no more veritable than his white man. Save for a sporadic play or two, a novel or an essay, the true psychic borderland of races between the Indian and the Caucasian is untouched. The Indian is a lay figure of melodrama; the white settler is a nasal, whining boor. A great spiritual region lies within reach of the hand of the new American dramatist.

And who knows the pioneer? He still lives in many of the newer parts of the country in healthy and prosperous retirement. His life has been one of exercise with body and mind in the open. He stands so close to many of us that we can hardly interpret him as yet. But the historians of America are beginning to know his value, and to see in him, in his restlessness, scorn of limitations, and moral cocksureness the true type of American. In some ways, and these the "common-sense" ways, the pioneer rose to genius as a type. He knew the discount-value of the future; therefore he had a humorous, long-lived patience; he was willing to wait, even to take his payment out in the promise of his sons' and grandsons' realization. One cannot study history without studying the psychology of men; certainly one cannot write plays without such study. When men people a wilderness within one generation, and build roads and walls and dykes, and clear the fields, in a political and social as well as a forest wilderness, there is a psychology lying behind them worthy of the study of the historian and the dramatist. If we could drop everything that is meant by the term "American" and retain the meaning of "pioneer," we should have lost nothing. The world would still be enriched by a heritage. It is a fallacy that treats the pioneer as simply a dealer in corner-lots. This he was, and in this activity we have much of the meaning of the term "American." But he was more than this. Had he not been more his corner-lots would not have increased in value. For it is no unearned increment that is now being collected on the lives and ideals and toil of the pioneers. The increment we are now gathering comes not only from the flocking of the hordes; it comes as well from the clear vision, the determination, the concrete poetizing in terms of new institutions in which the pioneers were adept. The pioneer was as apt at planting new institutions as he was in cutting down old ones. And always the institution he planted was one that could not conceivably flower in his own day, that could come to fruit only in the time of his sons and the sons of his sons. Yet he digged the soil and planted the trees. He had a wholesome trust in man's ability to save himself by his own formulas. If there was anything wrong or undone in the universe, let the correction be but expressed in an institution and things would come out right. He had not come to the truth that the institution itself could express society only as it is, and that the house that is builded will be as the builder himself. But this planting of institutions was not for nothing. For it was in the planting rather than in the tree he planted that the pioneer showed himself. The important thing was that the pioneer was a planter and a builder. He believed in the power of nature to make grow; and he believed in the power of his own arm to build up. He is not only a heritage; he is a Fact of American life. And the dramatist, searching for truth, the veritable truth that lies near at hand, will sometime find the pioneer, standing close by his own hearthstone, regnant, constructive, materially imaginative, and above all a believer. He will find him, and in his plays he will have an American.

It is said that we are a nation of city-builders. One who knows the country knows that this statement only partly covers the case; that the typical American spirit lies rather more near to the heart of the village than to the heart of the city. The real spirit of America lies in an ability to wait rather than in impatience, in a humorous gift of self-scrutiny, and in a belief in homely expedients. These are not city attributes. The cities are more noisy, but the villages are more quietly tenacious. If there is one force that more than anything else represents America it is neighborliness, in all the homespun value of the term. And neighborliness is an attribute of village life. Neighborliness is the product of pioneer days. It is a quality as native and simple as the American backgrounds. It has no ethical or hortatory or mawkish value. It is an outgrowth of the days when men were drawn together by common interest against the loneliness of their lives. In the world in which they lived there was plenty of everything save neighbors. To buy companionship they were free with material possessions. This developed a hospitality, a grace in giving, and an easy communicativeness.

Neighborliness means not only the development of the virtues of society. Neighborliness is no panacea; it never rises higher than humanity itself. But it does not pervert humanity; it shows men as they are.

Neighborliness permits the expression of the simpler vices as well as the simpler virtues. In the fences and the cliques, the jealousies and the gossip, the minding-of-everybody's-business of the small town, the drawbacks of village life are seen. But, at any rate, these are natural and human drawbacks, they are not the drawbacks of the inverted and attenuated life of the city. They are not laid over with the pressure of the city to disguise and conceal their true character under a pretense of social necessity or sophistication.

And so we would look for one type of the American play in the village. In the village there are people enough to reveal the true characteristics of our life, and not so many that these characteristics are crushed by weight of numbers. In the village there is a closeness to the background, a fidelity to type that the city cannot show. Where each man has his yard, surrounded with a fence which marks his precincts from those of his neighbor, where part of the day's work is the tending of the garden, perhaps of the cow, horse, or chickens, the structure of life is built on a base set in the instinctive and necessary. America has not yet risen above an identification with these instinctive supports of living. In spite of our boasted "civilization of expedients," it has been the province of America to simplify relationships by taking them back to the lowest terms, by making them inhere in homely things. Our greatest genius in the handling of subtle problems has risen from our ability to handle them ultimate meaning may be for art no one ventures even to guess.

There is one function that our cities are serving that seems to symbolize one of the largest meanings of the American democracy. The city has become the meeting-place and the welding-place of peoples of different races. It has been the fortune of America as a whole to create a new people out of the representatives of many older peoples. And to-day it is in the cities that the process of creation, of amalgamation, is centred. This process of interchange and readjustment is one of the eternal phenomena, and at the same time one of the mysteries, of human nature. To the dramatist it comes in two forms. To one dramatist, upon whose thinking the formulas of positivism and responsibility have been impressed, it comes as a problem of awful import, testing the resources of his mind and leading him to pessimism upon the theory that any problem that he cannot solve is without solution. This is the man who goes to the sociologist and the political scientist, and, thinking that the data they have already gathered is adequate to an understanding of man, proceeds to plot the curve of the future by the insufficient records of the past. To the other dramatist the eternal restless interplay of man upon the earth has its value as an unsolved and therefore majestic phenomenon, one of the greatest phenomena of the world, containing within it the mystery not only of origins, but of destiny, and the profound speculations of association and brotherhood and love. In retaining its mystery to him this phenomenon still retains its magnitudes. He has no vaunting desire to usurp great places or to hasten deliberate processes. He recognizes that the laws of the spirit are still all-powerful, and that what the reason cannot comprehend is still within the grasp of the simpler spirit. As a spiritual thing the mingling of the races comes to him, not as a problem with which, weak-handed as he is, he is expected to cope.

To the dramatist who is willing to take the city as a complex of mysterious forces of life it looms up in tremendous possibilities. In this nucleus are all the possibilities of experiment, perhaps even the achievement, of that thing called "understanding" among men. Here in small compass are the possibilities of unity without conformity, of the cultivation of the art of the individual life and the orchestration of men. The city is a rich mine for the dramatist who views it reverently. The world has never yet seen the city in its completeness. But to-day we are more nearly ready to accept the meaning of the city than we have ever been. Both on the side of thought and of material interchange we are ready for the message of the cities. Belief in the fluidity of ideas and the unity of the primary spirits of men was never so near acceptance as it is to-day. And on the material side the last two generations have brought to realization quick interchanges between nation and nation that have not shall run to dross. The art of America will be the art not of problems but of possibilities. We will not call upon our art to carry our burdens, and to whine with our discontents, but to discover us and reveal us for what we are.

With such materials as these, how is a dramatic art to be made? There will be little satisfaction in attempting to express it in the old forms and the old technique. For the substance of American drama is going to demand a style of its own, and the new materials will supply their own technique. This is said in no spirit of reform or iconoclasm. It is a conclusion based upon the observation of dramatic art under all circumstances, an observation that convinces one that form is of the very substance of dramatic art, and that the change of the one involves the change of the other. Certainly the form of the new American drama will not be based upon the old reactions of an age of chivalry, or on the restless anarchy of the breaking-up of the age of European castes. And it may lack some of the easy divisions and categories by which the clashes of the older drama were represented. As society becomes more balanced and coherent, the dramatist loses the easy formulas by which the play has been made. Instead of these the American dramatist will have to discover newer alignments, out of which will come a new technique.

There would be no value in attempting to state the formula of the new technique. If we state its source and

the motive that impels it, we will have done enough
to indicate what its form must be. The motive may be
the motive of the normal American village, expressed
in the temper of the pioneer spirit. The cohering power
of the play will lie in simple neighborliness, in crude
hanging together; the temper of the play will be that
laconic optimism, that sturdy imaginativeness that has
marked the first settlers. As to whether the play will be
long or short, plastic or ideal or intellectual, presented
in large theatres or small, through comedy or tragedy,
be broken into short acts and scenes or drawn out
in a single growing unit, whether the play will be
formalized in structure or rough and ready, I do not
venture to suggest, because I do not know. These
are matters of clothing in which styles change from
time to time without touching the steady course of
events.

Lest it be thought that the purpose of this book, and
particularly of this chapter, is the foretelling of future
events, a final word of explanation may be permitted.
Much that passes as prophecy is a bootless occupation.
But if by prophecy is meant the study of present tendencies, to discover their outcome in the light of their
principles and past history, then we are willing to accept the task of prophecy. For there is no undertaking so thoroughly fundamental as this. We have
thought that we could find in the study of the present
constitution of American society and of the organiza-

tion of the American theatre the faults of the relationship between the two. Mutually coexisting entities, one of which implies and involves the other, require this dual investigation. We have found many points at which the theatre fails to represent society; many points at which society fails to support the theatre. In such a case as this the fault is not of the one or the other. It is of the adjustment and relationship of the two.

In addition we have discovered certain demands on the part of society that are not satisfied by the theatre, and we have found that society is setting up processes to correct the faults and shortcomings of the theatre. In discovering social needs and demands we are discovering demands that in the course of nature must and will be satisfied. This is all that prophecy can safely do at any time. And if this be prophecy, then certainly prophecy has been elevated to a position among the sciences.

For we have here no argument or dream or promise of a bright but hardly to be realized future. No dramatic millennium lies just around the corner. If there has been read into this book any such promise, the author has failed to state his meaning. What has been meant is that an American drama must come in the nature of things; that processes are clearly discernible and at work that must bring it. No claim is made that the American drama when it arrives will save the world, or dispense with further problems of a material and spiritual nature. It will play the part it is called upon by its nature to play, the part for which it is created. If it is said that never before has an art era been promised with such bold assurance, the answer may be made that heretofore social processes have not been studied in the way in which they are now studied, have not, indeed, been held to be subject to inductive reasoning. To-day we do not question that man is governed by laws involved in his own constitution. Our only limitations, great enough to be sure, are the limitations of the understanding and knowledge of these laws.

And there is one further word. A nation cannot build a palace of art to live in any more than can a man. If art is to come, it must come not as a purposed creation apart from the fundamental motives of life, in which are spent only the leisure and the detached hours; it must come as a part of the body of society, as the outgrowth of the inherent processes of events; and it must be a house for the whole family, in which are carried forward all the activities of men. The idea of the palace of art has bred many hypocrisies and affectations. These are serious enough in old nations in which the arts are venerable. This idea may mean schools of art, and academies of styles, cults, and isms, and affectations, the parasites and the decadent growths of art. In old societies they are barnacles of established art; they do not dim the lustre of real achievement. But in new countries that have still to discover themselves they are more serious than this. With us they are the false show that by many is accepted as the true thing; they are works of the imitators and dilettantes who coin a nice stipend of fame from their spurious metal. They stand in the way of the quieter workman who is unused to the systems of exploitation; and flatter the senses of the inexpert by glitter and fine phrases. And in the more judicial-minded they breed a contempt for all that goes under the name of art.

Art is not of this sort. It is delicate, but it is hardy. It hides its head, but it has deep roots. It deals with the things of the spirit, but it has a firm grip on the things of the flesh. It is of the time and of the place. The true art is not ashamed of its paternity. We will know our art when it comes by the fact that it is American through and through. It is American in no apologetic mood, as one should say, "better things are to follow," or, "it is as good as could be expected under the circumstances," or, "like parent like child"; but with a sane pride, a healthy self-veneration that comes from a knowledge of the truth and of the instruments with which one searches for truth, of one who knows that he works with his full strength, sleeps deeply, and awakes glad of a new day.

The American art will not be ashamed of the dollar, or be ashamed of a certain frank moral opportunism which takes the tasks of each day and does them with the strength of the day, or ashamed (and still not proud) of a certain roughness and largeness of hand-clasp, or ashamed of something of palpability in our sentiment and humor. These things are American, for they are of our own nature. May we expect plays to come of them? Let us try and see.

THE END

The Riverside Press
CAMBRIDGE . MASSACHUSETTS
U . S . A